Dear J,

You, too, [on]
this journey to find
my voice and courage.
I am deeply grateful.

Gaby

© 2019 Cynthia M. Ruiz, Gabriela Torres, Jennie Estrada, Anita L.Sanchez, Ph.D., Abel Salas, Brenda Xavez, Suki Eaton, Gena Contreras, Chella Diaz and Lorraine Martinez Cook

All stories are copyrights of their respective owners and are used with permission.

The Yo Tambien Healing Movement logo is a service and tradmark of Cynthia M. Ruiz, Jennie Estrada and Gabriela Torres.

All rights reserved. No portion of this book may be reproduced in any form without permission from the authors, except as permitted by U.S. copyright law. For permissions contact:

yotambienhealing@gmail.com

Cover by Michelle Niellose.

Yo También Stories of Healing & Hope
ISBN number 9781095690239

ACKNOWLEDGMENTS

This book has been a labor of love, and we are grateful to anyone who has helped us along the way.

The Yo También Healing movement would like to acknowledge the ten brave souls that stepped up and shared their story in this book, and we accept those who were not quite ready.

We send Love to the entire community, which supports each of us on our journeys.

We want to give a special shout out to the fantastic photographer Steve Lucero for the group photo used on the back cover. And one to Michelle Niellose for the beautiful artistry in the design of our logo and in the layout of our book.

Check out Steve's work at:
STEVE LUCERO PHOTOGRAPHY
www.SteveLucero.com

and Michelle's work at:
Michelle Niellose
@ @michelleniellose

YO TAMBIÉN HEALING MOVEMENT INTRODUCTION

We have united to take a stand against sexual abuse in the Latino Community. We are here to facilitate healing of all people, which have experienced sexual trauma. We can no longer sit on the sidelines we need to become change agents to unite the community and put an end to the cycle of emotional destruction. We believe in healing, We believe in Love, and We know when people come together anything is possible.

Our mission is to create a platform within the Latino Community for the primary purpose of facilitating healing from sexual trauma. The vision is to build a movement to develop a community of healing and hope, using a holistic healing model of mind, body & spirit

Sexual trauma is a topic that has been taboo because it has been too painful to discuss. However, by ignoring the problem, the cycle continues, and the next generation will experience the same agony.

It is a subject that as a society we have not discussed until very recently with the wave of the "Me too" movement. The Me Too movement has opened the floodgates and catapulted the conversation to the forefront of the news. Many influential individuals are now being held accountable for their actions.

Depending on whom you listen to, 1 out of every 5 women in the US will be sexually abused in her life. For men, the number is 1 in 12. That means if you have not experienced the trauma yourself you know someone who has, a friend or family member. It is incumbent upon all of us to come together to allow a safe space for the healing process to begin. Healing not only as an individual but also as a society.

According to the US Department of Justice, only 16% of all rapes are reported to law enforcement. Some people don't understand why victims don't report the incident to authorities right away. The answer is complicated, and many times the person feels victimized again when they come forward and speak out.

In the Latino community, no one has been able to get accurate numbers since it is not even discussed let alone reported. It is further complicated since a family member or family friend usually causes the trauma. Frequently the injury occurs before the age of eighteen, not only to girls but boys as well.

We each have a story, and no two stories are the identical. Many stories have commonalities, and we hope that there is something in these stories that will resonate with you and inspire you to take action to heal from the trauma you have experienced. You do not have to endure the pain any longer; you have the choice to be free.

If you have loved ones around you who have experienced the hurt share this book with them and we hope it will help them as they travel the road to wholeness.

We believe the healing will not only help people today, but it will pave the way for future generations so they will not have to experience the physical and emotional pain so many have endured. Some never recover and find the only way out is self-sabotage or suicide.

This is a cycle that must be broken, and as a community, we need to be a part of the solution.

We share these stories with you with the intention of healing and providing hope.

DISCLAIMER
This is not a formula or prescription for healing, these are our own individual stories.

We ask you to stand with us...

THE YO TAMBIÉN HEALING MOVEMENT FOUNDERS

GABRIELA TORRES · JENNIE ESTRADA · CYNTHIA M RUIZ

CONTENTS

9 **The Path to Freedom: Breaking the Shackles of the Past**
Cynthia M. Ruiz

33 **On Returning to Myself After Rape**
Gabriela Torres

55 **Believing Matters**
Jennie Estrada

63 **The Four Sacred Gifts:
Personal and Spiritual Growth After Trauma**
Anita L. Sanchez, PhD

89 **The Truth is That**
Abel Salas

119 **Mi Testimonio: A Story of Survival and Healing**
Brenda Xavez

147 **My Self Discovery of Inner Strength**
Suki Eaton

165 **Warrior Mother**
Gena Contreras

185 **Hiding In Plain Sight**
Chella Diaz

203 **Where Do We Go from Here?**
Lorraine Martinez Cook

210 **Yo También Healing Movement Contact Info**

"Growth is a painful process. If we're ever going to collectively begin to grapple with the problems that we have collectively, we're going to have to move back the veil and deal with each other on a more human level."

Wilma Mankiller
Principle Chief Cherokee Nation

CYNTHIA M. RUIZ
Author, Professor, Executive Coach, Leadership Expert, Mother & Latina Influencer

Receiving over 50 accolades and awards for her leadership and service, Cynthia currently serves as the President of the LACERS Board (Los Angeles City Employees Retirement System) overseeing a multibillion-dollar pension.

Hispanic Lifestyle Magazine named her a "2018 Latina of Influence". She is a co-founder of the Yo También Healing Movement. Cynthia has over twenty years of teaching experience and is a successful entrepreneur. She always finds time to give back to the community by mentoring, teaching and empowering others.

Coming from blended cultures Mexican & Cherokee, she enjoys a passion for life and a profound appreciation for Mother Earth.

www.CynthiaMRuiz.com

PATH TO FREEDOM
BREAKING THE SHACKLES OF THE PAST

It is another beautiful day in the City of the Angels, the sun is shining bright, and the temperature is perfect. I feel a gentle breeze brush across my face as if the ancestors are awakening me from my deep meditation.

As my eyes slowly open the first thing I see is the enormous, beautiful tree, which I sit next to when I meditate in my back yard. Her name is Luna - a name, which was given to her during one of our full moon ceremonies since she is the anchor connecting us to the heartbeat of Mother Earth. The tree is wise, and her roots travel deep into the soil, which helps me feel grounded, centered and protected.

As my eyes continue to focus, I begin to be filled with love and gratitude. I truly appreciate how blessed I am to be alive. I realize that my life is rich with unbelievable experiences and so many amazing people uplifting me with unconditional love.

The smile on my face widens as I reminiscence on my life's journey, the trials, and tribulations which have shaped the woman I am today. As a child, I would often dream of the future, but those dreams were limited by my upbringing, today's reality has exceeded all my childhood expectations. I was always driven to help other people yet was not sure how I would accomplish such a task.

My mind begins to wander and I start to reflect on my life but it does not stop there I begin to think about the women in my family who have paved the way for me. The women who have previously traveled this earth and allowed me to stand on the strength of their shoulders.

My maternal grandmother, Joanna was born in Indian Territory in 1896 and was a woman of few words. She never shared with me that her mother had died when she was only four years old, and she was raised by her step-mother. Her homeland became the State of Oklahoma in 1907 when grandmother was eleven. She carried with her the unimaginable pain the Cherokee people endured during the "Trail of Tears" when they were forcibly removed from their home. Marching from the Carolinas through the extreme cold to be placed in an unfamiliar land. Thousands of people died along the terrifying journey not only from the radical elements but also from disease, which was brought to them by the intruders. I learned the lesson of humility from my grandmother.

My thoughts then turn to my paternal grandmother, Encarnacion who started her journey in Sinaloa Mexico coming to Los Angeles in 1922 with my grandfather, a 4-month-old baby girl, and a six-year-old stepson. She went on to bear nine more children and unfortunately had to experience the unimaginable pain of losing one of her sons. She left the physical world when I was only five years old but instilled in me kindness, which I carry with me today.

My mind then begins to focus on my life. My earliest memories are filled with intense physical pain not from external sources but my own body. At age three I was diagnosed with clubfeet and wore orthopedic shoes for several years to correct the problem.

The pain followed me, and later all the doctor could tell my mom was, "They were growing pains." That provided little comfort to me during the nights when the pain would become so intense all I could do was to weep. I remember asking myself what did I do to cause this agony. Was the doctor right? Was it growing pains? Or did my ancestors pass the pain to me? Maybe it was meant to make me stronger so I could face what was ahead.

I grew up in Los Angeles in a turbulent household where my parents were always fighting, mostly verbal yet occasionally physical. Both parents were passionate people, which created the unsettling environment. Passion can be a good thing, but when it is layered on an unstable foundation and alcohol, it can become unpredictable and scary for a young child.

My father was a Latin Jazz musician and played percussions: drums, timbales, and congas. In addition to his day job at a loan company, he worked late nights at various nightclubs. My mom constantly accused him of cheating and being a womanizer, which was at the core of most of their arguments. As a young girl, I had no idea if that was true or what it even meant.

Out of their four children, I was the only girl and had a solid bond with my Dad. I was "daddy's little girl" so I usually took his side in their fights which did not sit well with my mother. Honestly, I don't think I really understood what was going on, I just remember there being a lot of yelling and cursing and I wanted it to stop. There was always tension in the household and very few happy memories when we lived together as a family unit.

There was no escape until one day my uncle built us a tree house in our backyard. Once the tree house was made, I had a place to hide and be a kid. Even as a young girl I knew my ancestors surrounded me, I believed they were guiding me and knew I was not alone.

By the time my Mom delivered her fourth child she was so upset and anxious all of the time my youngest brother was born prematurely. He was in the hospital for about a month before he was allowed to come home. Very shortly after that, my parents separated.

I was seven years old when my parents filed for a divorce. Being the only girl, I had to grow up fast and pitch in caring for my baby brother. I still can remember changing his diapers and giving him his bottle even though I was just a child myself.

On some level, I was happy when my parents divorced since the fighting stopped. The flip side was, it threw my mom into a tailspin, which I am not sure she ever fully recovered. I believe my dad was the love of her life and although she went on to remarry, she carried the hurt with her. Because I had always sided with my dad, my Mother never forgave me and treated me adversely all of my life until she was diagnosed with dementia a few years ago.

My parents had a very traditional marriage, and my Mom never worked outside the home so after the divorce she was forced to go on welfare for a short period. She worked hard to make sure that was a temporary situation.

She had four kids to care for and was doing the best she could. She obtained basic office training so she could get a job. Once she received some skills, she was able to land a job with the County of Los Angeles where she stayed until she retired. My Mother worked her way up into management and most of her career she served as the liaison to the Native American Community. That was a very challenging role, but she somehow managed to be effective.

Once my parents divorced, things at home stabilized for a little while, and my mom married for a second time. Due to the fact that her world was limited, she became romantically involved with the neighbor. My stepfather was a hard-working man who spent his days employed as a machinist and his nights at the local bar. There were many times my mom would go check on him because of the lack of trust, which carried over from her first marriage. She would drag me along and since I was underage and could not go in. I would be left in the bar's kitchen waiting for her for what seems like hours at a time, and maybe it was.

At home, I was a tomboy playing with my brothers and their friends. I saw my dad every other weekend. That is on the weekends he decided to show up which turned out to be sporadic at best, there would be many times I would sit there waiting for him heartbroken when I realized he was a no-show. That created an emotional roller coaster with the highs of spending time with him and the lows of disappointment.

When we were together, we would listen to music, mostly jazz. This laid the foundation for my profound appreciation for music.

He also remarried for a second time to a woman who had a child from a previous relationship they soon had a son together. Now in addition to my three brothers, I had a half-brother and a stepbrother. Not to mention three more stepsiblings from my stepfather. Needless to say, it was a complicated question when people asked me if I had any siblings.

Unfortunately, my dad's second marriage ended in divorce, and I have not had any communication with my half brother.

My dad's longest relationship ended up being his third marriage, which lasted until he left this earth. His third wife never had any children of her own, so she discouraged my Father from having any relationship with us, which he obliged. During the last twenty- five years of his life he chose his marriage over his children and moved away with no forwarding address.

A few months before he passed at age 84, he called me out of the blue at my work. He asked if he could borrow some money and gave me a P.O. Box in Chula Vista to send it to. Of course, I sent him the money and told him it was a gift, not a loan. I did, however, take advantage of the opportunity to express my displeasure at not seeing him for all those years. I was sad over the fact he had not gotten to know my son, his grandson. Once my Father received my letter, he voided the check and sent it back and had no further communication.

Even as a young girl I had an entrepreneurial spirit always looking for ways to make money. Starting at age twelve or thirteen I would babysit for families around my neighborhood. It was something I enjoyed, and I certainly liked having money to buy records and clothes.

When I was fourteen years old, my mom came home from work and proclaimed she had a co-worker who needed a babysitter. I jumped on the opportunity and was already thinking about what I would buy with the money I made.

My mom dropped me off at the couple's house, and when we arrived, I was surprised when they announced they wanted me to spend the night. I was caught off guard but agreed once they explained it would be too late for them to drive me home. My mom said she would be back the next morning to pick me up.

The couple went out, and I had a great evening caring for the young boy who was around two. I put him to bed and proceeded to settle in for the night on their living room couch where they had left a blanket and pillow for me to be comfortable.

I have always been a sound sleeper and didn't even hear them when they came home. I began to dream, and to my surprise, it was a sensual dream, which started to stimulate my body with pleasure.

In a split second the dream turned into a nightmare when I woke up to find the husband was the source of the stimulation. I tried to scream, but he covered my mouth with his hand. I was fourteen, and he was in his mid-thirties. I was surprised, confused and scared all at the same time. I started to put up a fight, so he eventually gave up and retreated back into his bedroom and closed the door.

It then became the longest night of my life, I lay awake all night shaking and softly crying. The next morning my Mom came to pick me up, and I could not get out of there soon enough. The entire car ride I sat in silence. Once we got home, I locked myself in my room and cried.

A few weeks later my mom came home from work and announced I would be going back to the couples house for another babysitting job. I didn't want to go back and told my Mom no.

She said, "Well too bad I already told them you would do it." I tried to tell my mom what happened but the words would not come out, my mom insisted. She is a very stubborn person and always got her way.

The second time I babysat for this family, I was so afraid I didn't sleep a wink, and the situation repeated itself. He did not take no for an answer.

I did not feel comfortable enough to tell my Mom what happened, as I feared she would blame me. I was nauseated, repulsed and afraid of this man who was more than twice my age. I felt violated.

The third time the couple wanted me to babysit I put my foot down and refused to go. My mom was furious with me and screamed that I was being ungrateful, but I knew I could not endure another night.

Surprisingly my mom never asked why I didn't want to go back, she knew I continued to babysit for other families. She was more worried about disappointing her friends rather than wanting to know what I was feeling. I did get in trouble and was grounded for a month for disobeying her, but I didn't care because anything was better than being placed in that situation again.

I continued to work various part-time jobs and was always good at saving money my philosophy was paying my bills, saving money and having fun with the rest. My mom and I continued to have a rocky relationship, and after one of her meltdowns, she became physically violent with me, so I moved out and at the tender age of seventeen. I became roommates with a girlfriend.

I had just graduated from high school, and I was getting ready to start college in the fall. It was uncharted territory since I was the first person in my family to attend a university. That summer was filled with fun and new adventures, yet at the same time I was trying to fend for myself without the support of anyone and was doing the best I could.

That summer my life changed forever when the unthinkable happened to me. I was violently raped and never saw it coming. It was by someone who I had known for a short period, a guy that I had actually liked. He was in his twenties, good looking and guess what he was a musician. He threatened me and said if I told anyone he would kill me and after what occurred I believed him.

I was feeling so many emotions all at once: anger, shame, guilt, humiliation, and disdain. I drove myself home but everything was a blur, and I jumped in the shower as soon as I walked in the door since I felt dirty. I didn't tell anyone other than my roommate, I did not even think of calling the police or filing a police report. I did not see them as anyone who could protect me.

The possibility of retaliation stayed with me despite that fact the perpetrator did not know where I lived. The fear overruled my logical mind, and I was petrified he would find me. The thought of having to see him again made me sick, so I stayed quiet and kept my mouth shut.

The shock and disbelief bubbled in the back of my mind leaving me with a feeling of uneasiness and not feeling safe, which remained with me for many years. I could not believe someone could do something so terrible to me, it was the first time in my life I could actually remember feeling true fear. This fear was 100 times worst then what I felt before.

The physical wounds healed within a few weeks but the emotional scars stayed with me. The incident played in my mind over and over again like a broken record. I always wondered if I could have done something different to avoid the situation. I also questioned what I had done to have such a terrible thing happen to me. In some strange way, I thought I was responsible.

I moved forward with my life the best I could and that September when I started college I focused on my schoolwork, so I didn't have to think about it. Using the only defense mechanism I knew, I buried my feelings and found comfort living in denial.

Since I went to local college, I continued to live with my roommate until she found a boyfriend and decided to move in with him. I managed to keep the two-bedroom apartment and lived off of the money I earned from working two jobs, students loans and grants.

I assumed my life had returned to normal. However those deep emotions of not feeling safe haunted me. It was if I had a dark stain on my soul.

The first few years of college were demanding, and it required adjusting to a new life. I became involved in social justice issues thinking I was going to change the world. During those activities, I met another student but was hesitant to get involved in any relationship given my past experience.

After a year of casually knowing him I had hosted a meeting at my apartment and well he never left. I didn't question it since I didn't like living alone, I can see now that it was my feeling of uneasiness, which allowed the relationship to move so quickly.

We started living together when I was just 19 years old. We married three years later after I graduated from the university with my Bachelors of Arts degree. I was determined to break the cycle of the past, so I continued my education and obtained my Master's Degree.

I knew if I got an education it would provide me the independence to never be finically reliant on another person. This was rooted in what I had seen my Mother go through after divorcing my dad.

My experience of sexual trauma stayed inside me even though I thought I had buried it. On the outside, I was a cheerful college student but on the inside had this nagging feeling that would not go away so I continued to stuff that discomfort down as far as I possibility could.

At one point I share what happened to me with my husband. It made him very uncomfortable, and he did not know what to say so we never discussed it again. He had his own demons from his past, and I found myself in a physically abusive marriage and felt trapped.

My career began to thrive, and I found my job to be a safe place, so I began to work more. As my energy was funneled into my career, the trauma laid dormant.

The duality of my life caused internal conflict, and I didn't know how to dull the pain of the sexual and then physical abuse. Just like the past, I did not tell anyone. I knew that if my brothers found out, it would definitely cause drama. So the new hurt was being heaped on top of my previous experiences.

The bright spot during this period in my life was the birth of my son, a vibrant baby filled with life and possibilities. The unconditional love from my son was soothing, and the success of my career gave me pride.

The secret of the physical abuse finally came out ten years into the marriage when he exploded in front of our friends, and I could no longer hide it. It took me some time to let go of that relationship since we had a business together as well as our child.

Once I got divorced, I shared joint custody of my seven-year-old son; we had a 50/50 split on our time. I had to quickly become responsible for raising him on my own and healing myself.

My self-esteem had been so damaged by the marriage I questioned myself in all areas of my life. So what did I do? Jumped into the first relationship, which came along. That also proved to be a very unhealthy relationship and a roller coaster ride of highs and lows, which lasted off and on for seven years.

Once I decided to get off the roller coaster, I realized that I needed to work on myself. It was time to start the healing process from the pain I had been avoiding all those years.

My degrees were in counseling, so I had always been a fan of self-help and motivational books. I would read books and listen to CDs. At that time I found those sources to be motivational but not really spiritual. I was still seeking something more significant.

My ability to set goals and execute them kept me on track to reach the things I wanted in life. I also found it was easier for me to give to others than turn within and face my darkness. I incorporated giving back to the community and others as a way of life. It gave me joy and made me feel good.

My life continued to thrive; yet I continued to feel fragmented. Most of the time I was happy but tucked away in the abyss of my unconsciousness was that pestering dull ache.

My spiritual journey allowed me to connect with my ancestors, the Creator, and my true authentic self. I was able to begin shedding the pain from the past. It was a slow process but necessary if I was going to find the inner peace I had been longing for.

The healing journey was a winding road with ups and downs, twist and turns. Just when I felt it was in the rearview mirror something popped up.

Today I have found inner peace by taking one step at a time, believing in myself and never giving up. I always knew that eventually, I would arrive at my secure place. The destination was freedom from the trauma, which kept me shackled to my past.

My focus turns to the present and as I look around my backyard and I can now see the warm glow of the sunset. I once again am wrapped in the feeling of love and not being alone, as I know those who have traveled this earth before me are by my side. I have the awareness that the challenges, which I have faced, are stepping-stones into the future. A future that involves helping others find their freedom.

Yes, it is another perfect day in the City of the Angels as I sit in the understanding that my life's journey is perfect just the way it is.

SPIRITUALITY AS MY PATH TO EMOTIONAL FREEDOM

I have always believed in God. Coming from blended cultures (Latina & Native American) I also use the term Creator. Although I did not participate in organized religion growing up, I did pray. Prayer would somehow make me feel safe.

The more connected I felt to the Creator, the easier my life became. I would go with the flow of life having the conviction that everything would be all right. My faith allowed me to keep moving forward even though I was not entirely sure of what was going to happen next.

I also found comfort when I was surrounded by Nature and hiked on a regular basis. Being with Mother Nature provides me grounded energy, which I find essential for my well-being.

I consider myself very spiritual not necessarily religious. It is the Creator, which lead me down my path of healing. I do incorporate a spiritual practice in my daily routine.

PRAYER ON A DAILY BASIS

Prayer has been a great tool in my healing process. I pray on a daily basis, I don't have a specified amount of time nor do I get down on my knees. I can be driving, sitting in my back yard or hiking.

I consider prayer to be talking to God; it is not about the structure it is about what feels right to you. If you believe like I do that God is omnipresent, you will realize your prayers will be heard wherever you are.

Several years ago I took a prayer class, and for our homework, I was challenged to write my own prayer. At first, I was not sure how I felt about the assignment.

I always thought you had to be a Saint, Reverend or Pastor to do so. But then I remembered that a "Prayer" is just talking to God, so I wrote down my thoughts. I embraced the exercise and was happy with the results, in fact, I added my Prayer to the end both of my books.

So when you pray you can use traditional prayers but don't be afraid just to have a conversation with God. To talk about what is on your mind and in your heart.

MEDITATION IS A PART OF MY SPIRITUAL PRACTICE.

For many people in the Latino, community meditation is a foreign concept. It is something that did not come easily to me and took me many years to be comfortable doing. Until I realized that mediation is a complement to prayer. Just like I believe prayer is talking to God, I think that meditation is listening to God. In the stillness, you can receive the answers you seek.

When I first started to meditate, I would sit down and could not turn off my thoughts. I started thinking about what I needed to do and began working on my "to-do" list. So I decided to take a guided meditation class where the instructor would gently guide us using music and visualizations. I started to become more comfortable and would focus on her voice and not what I needed to do when I finished the class.

As I have progressed the stillness of meditation is a safe place of bliss. It is my safe haven away from the hustle and bustle of urban life.

GRATITUDE

Today my mantra in life is, "I am blessed and Grateful, and gratitude is a big part of my daily life. I start my day with my gratitude list, which helps me set a positive tone for the day. When I wake up in the morning I think about the things I am grateful for, I am thankful to have a bed to sleep in, a roof over my head and the unconditional love of so many amazing people.

I am grateful to share my story and optimistic that it will give you a path forward towards your healing allowing you to live a life filled with love and joy.

If you have not experienced sexual abuse or sexual trauma, I am sure you know someone who has, and my desire is you can help him or her by starting the uncomfortable conversation. The awkward conversation is the first phase of the healing process.

MY HEALING PROCESS

If you take the time to invest in your own healing, you will harvest the rewards.

I share the steps that worked for me knowing that what works may be different.

There is not a right way or wrong way, there is your way. It does not matter how you get to the place of healing what matters is that you start the journey.

5 STEPS TO HEALING:
Acknowledge what happened.
Forgive the person.
Forgive yourself.
Release the experience.
Accept your uniqueness & learn to love yourself.

STEP 1 Acknowledge what happened

It is the process of moving from denial to acknowledgment, saying it out loud to yourself or someone you can trust.

As simple as this step sounds it was probably the most challenging thing I had to do. I had to acknowledge my secret, something that I concealed for so many years. I had to let all of those emotions rise to the top and it started by me admitting to myself that I had been raped.

Despite that fact, many years had passed I somehow remembered every detail like it just happened yesterday. After speaking with others, I realized that I was not alone. They can tell you what they were wearing, the day of the week, like if the experience became frozen and itched into their memory.

Once I actually said it out loud, there was no turning back. Then it became easier to repeat it. The initial shock of saying it became less and less painful. Now I talk about it when I speak in front of groups of people. I even made it a part of my speech while speaking at a women's conference to over 300 people. After I left the stage, I had a line of people waiting to talk with me wanting to share their story.

STEP 2 Forgive the Person, which caused the trauma.

Forgiveness is for your benefit, not the person that caused the damage.

I was aware that forgiveness was going to set me free from the person who had stolen my happiness so many years before.

I sat down and wrote a letter to him saying that I forgave him. I knew he would never read it since I had no intentions of sending it to him or even know his whereabouts.

Once I completed the letter, written with many tears I used a white candle and burned it. It was very cathartic as I watched the smoke go up in the air like the universe was taking away my pain. I used a white candle since white represents purity.

Forgiveness may also be needed for other people that you perceived of not protecting you from the trauma. This could be an adult in your life, family, teachers, coaches, etc. You may need to write them a letter as well and release it. If you do not want to burn the letter, you can shred it, cut it up, bury it or just throw it in the trash.

After completing the processes that nagging pain was still there along with the uneasiness of not feeling safe.

STEP 3 Forgive yourself.

Release the shame, guilt or self- blame.

Somehow I had internalized the experience and weirdly blamed myself, which I believe is a common occurrence. Victims feel that it is somehow their fault, the clothes they were wearing or being in a particular situation. I think the idea is perpetuated by society. I can look back now on the experience and say of course it was not my doing. No one deserves to be forced against his or her will.

Subconsciously I had internalized it without even knowing it. So at the point, I was able to forgive myself I found my sense of freedom and was able to mend the pain in my soul, which had kept me attached to my past.

I said out loud, "It was not my fault, and I release any emotions that support that false belief including, shame, guilt or self-blame."

STEP 4 Release the experience, so you are no longer attached to it.

Emotions have an energetic quality that stays in our body until we actually release the experience. How do you release the experience?

Similar to forgiveness I had to write it down. You go into as much detail as you feel comfortable with. I didn't go into a lot of detail I just wrote down, "I release the experience of being raped forever and it no longer has power over me." I then took the piece of paper and burnt it, just like before.

STEP 5 Accept your uniqueness & learn to love yourself.

Everyone is unique, and no two people are exactly the same. Just like our fingerprints, we are all different.

Once you accept your uniqueness and understand that you are perfect with all of your imperfections you can release your insecurities and know that you are beautiful or handsome on the inside and outside.

Use positive affirmations to proclaim:

>"I am perfect just the way I am"
>"I love myself "
>"I am worthy"
>"I am loveable"

Say it as often as you like until you believe it. Write it down and leave yourself love notes.

I have healed and you can too.

You are loveable and perfect just the way you are. so set yourself free!

"The wound is the place where the light enters you."

Rumi

GABRIELA TORRES
Communicator, Healer, Magical Human Being

Inspired by so many stories, I became a co-founder the Yo También Healing Movement to create space for connection. This journey reminds me that I am no one and everyone all at once. That words have the power to heal and that service to the community uplifts us all. I have a long career in social issues, communications and marketing. I am a graduate of Woodbury University and California State Los Angeles, a partner of Momentum Solutions Team, a professional coach and Reiki master. I am eternally grateful to a magical group of souls, near and far, who I deeply love.

www.mujermagica.com

ON RETURNING TO MYSELF AFTER RAPE

Flipping through the story of my life, you will find I have rape listed as chapter within it. At the beginning of this passage, I was a perfectly normal twenty-something going about her life, building a career, dating, and pondering life's questions about marriage, children, and the future. Then, in one night, everything changed. Everything inside and around me broke. And the darkness that came with that night did not lift for a very long time.

Although I continued to live my life as if nothing had ever happened, I was no longer the same person. The light had gone out of my eyes, my smile was a squiggly line of confusion, my insides were in a constant state of panic, and I felt like I had lost my voice. And I had. I spent a lot of time deep in the trenches of my broken places. It would be years before I could bring myself to begin the rebuilding process, but I did. And now, as I continue this ongoing journey of reconstruction and restoration, I want to share a couple of thoughts and lessons that continue to help. And I want you to know that you will walk through it, you will find your smile again and you will feel love again.

If sharing my journey means that those of you carrying a similar burden find even just a small ray of light, support and connection from reading it, then the discomfort and ache of recounting it will have been worth it. In this moment of a sacred exchange, I hope that what I share will make the weight on your own shoulders a little less heavy. I started the true healing process two years after the incident. I was prompted by, of all things, a jury duty summons. Until that point, I had been living in a state of denial. Survival mode had become my new version of "normal." After a morning of sitting and waiting for my assignment, I was called into the courtroom to be interviewed by the attorneys handling the case. The judge proceeded to tell us that it was a domestic violence dispute. In that moment, something happened in my body that I still cannot correctly identify, but which I now refer to as a detonator for my trauma triggers. I place the things, moments, and people that set off emotional memory bombs in this category.

I don't remember what I said when I was called up to be interviewed. I wasn't myself and nothing I verbally spoke remains in my memory. I don't know what expression I had on my face, what I looked like, or how I responded to the questions. I don't even remember walking out of the courthouse. What I do remember is the judge quietly asking me if I was alright, and if I needed assistance. I silently shook my head. I was not alright.

I went home and fell apart, quietly. I had to be "normal." As the memories of that night washed over me like an icy cold bucket of water, I felt myself falling into depression. It, quite literally, knocked me off my feet. I didn't get out of bed for about a month. I left only when I absolutely had to do something—go to the bathroom, attend class, eat with my family (though I mostly just played with my food). I didn't really want to eat, much less socialize. But I gained about forty pounds in the years that followed. It sounds random now, but that jury summons cracked open the opportunity to look into myself, into the incident, and to begin to build a path toward healing.
To this day, some—ahem—years later (I am now a woman

of a certain age), I continue to restore and heal. Because those of us with this shared experience spend so much time in a place of darkness, I decided to write this piece from a place where the light at the end of the tunnel could be seen. Because you will see the light at the end of the tunnel. Although the tone of my story may sound peppy and optimistic during certain parts of this chapter, please know that it has not been easy. Recounting this part of my life has been an ordeal for me. I don't want to minimize the pain, but I don't want to live there either. I am alive and there are things I want to do, goals to meet, love to give, and places to see! Rape is a part of my story; it is not my whole story.

My healing journey has been an interesting road, with bumps and new adventures that continue to lead me to a path of love and compassion—though I have to remind myself of this some days. Yes: love and compassion, especially toward myself. Honestly, that has been the hardest part. Shame, denial, anger—feeling and living in all that was easy. Finding ways to feel like me again, refusing to judge myself for any little imperfection and to feel worthy of good things—these were the real struggles. In the back of my mind there was a lingering voice that kept saying "you are damaged." For a very long time, it was loud and all I could hear.

The counterbalance to that voice was the collection of actions, big and small, that I took every day to renew my spirit. Even if it was the simple act of getting out of bed. I found strength where I thought there was none left. I have dared to fall in love when I thought I couldn't trust anymore. Allies and comfort came from the most unexpected people and places.

It has not been easy or rosy, but I'm here. In this place of courage (and sometimes, sheer will) joy, with an open heart (most of the time), a little wiser (I hope) and still as imperfect as ever, perhaps a little more gentle (I think). I walked this world with my secret for such a long time, feeling all kinds of things, often unhappy and scared, hiding behind a happy face. Only when I started to share this secret in a sacred exchange of stories, did I learn that there were so many of us walking around with deep wounds in various stages of repair and healing. It has been a little more than 20 years since I had this experience, and sometimes the act of remembering still brings tears (like now, as I sit here writing this).

As with any experience, healing does not happen overnight, and it is a daily intentional practice. Different years have required different methods, channels, and even people for my process to continue to move forward. And it is all okay. It is all necessary. Even the not-so-great parts, even when I wasn't so nice. All of it brought me closer to being myself and helped me grow as a person—though I curse a lot, am occasionally judgmental, morph into a totally different person behind the wheel, still can't keep my house organized, and constantly have to remind myself to breathe.

ON FINDING ALLIES AND COMFORT

The sacred exchange. Also known as random acts of connection, because no matter how we try to isolate ourselves, we can't get through this alone.

Every healing stage of this experience has brought new allies into my life. The sacred exchange, as I have come to call the sharing of sexual assault stories between those of us who have that life experience, has been surprising, humbling, and cathartic.

I want to clarify that for this part of the story, allies and comfort do not include my immediate circle of friends and family. I had already told most of them of my experience, and their love and support created the space and strength I needed to share this part of my life with the world. In these next paragraphs, I refer to those who unknowingly or unexpectedly demonstrated qualities I needed to learn, remember, and trust again. Here are three examples:

ALLIES In the first few years of healing, whether I was aware I was in the healing process or not, my allies were mostly the men who were either in, or coming into, my life. Consciously or subconsciously, I sought out male— and only male—friendships. I also developed a hard, masculine approach to life. It was the not-so-great side of masculinity—overtly invested in portraying emotional distance in a misplaced attempt to protect myself, a rigid denial of my own feminine qualities, especially the softer sides of compassion. All muscle, no heart. If I had no feelings, I couldn't feel hurt. I drank, smoked cigars, and refused to let anyone into my personal space. I wanted to travel in a pack of masculinity so that no man could hurt me. From my defensive and distressed frame of reference, it made sense. And it worked for quite a while. Men became my allies. A few, unknowingly, also became casualties in my internal war.

COMFORT As time passed, I began to be more comfortable with sharing my story. When I felt safe, when it was appropriate, and only within an intimate conversation. I didn't set up a soap box and use a megaphone to shout to the world, although there were times when I wanted to do that, too. What transpired in these conversations was incredibly beautiful, and occasionally shocking and humbling. Nine times out of ten, I was witness to someone else's story of sexual assault. These sacred exchanges happened in the most random places and situations. Half the time, I didn't start the conversation on that topic. It happened at bars, at parties, with acquaintances, with friends, with co-workers, with strangers, with people I admired, and with people who rubbed me the wrong way or pissed me off. I took particular care with connections I formed with this last group, and they became especially meaningful to me. During my moments with them, I understood why they were difficult. I must have been a big pain myself at times, too. We were wounded. We were angry.

So many sacred exchanges across the years. Some with recent experiences, some with long-held secrets. A funny thing started to happen: I began to recognize this pain in people's eyes before they ever even spoke a word to me. In a way, I felt like we were seeking each other out to feel validated, to feel understood, to be seen and accepted and loved without judgment.

ALLIES AND COMFORT

Along the way, I also found allies and comfort in my belly dance sisters. I registered to join a series of adult dance classes in our local parks and recreation system. I needed to lose weight, and this seemed like a fun way to get some exercise. Little did I know how deeply this would help in my healing. Here I was, participating in a circle of femininity and sensuality—and I was safe! Slowly, dance step by dance step, I began to reconnect with my own femininity and sensuality. During those first few years of self-blame, it was those two attributes that I had prosecuted, convicted, and imprisoned somewhere in my mind as the reasons why I was raped. I know I had NO fault in this and still... I don't think this group of dancers will ever know how deeply they have impacted my life. We were all of different ethnicities, sizes, ages, and faiths, but in this dance group we were one rhythm and it was beautiful and sparkly. And for the first time in a long time I felt I could be beautiful and sparkly, too. Once more, I could be that.

ON FALLING IN LOVE WITH MY PHYSICAL BODY.
Again. And again. And again. Because really, that act of self-love takes effort, particularly for those of us who have sexual trauma in their life experience.

I came to dislike my physical body a lot. I didn't hate it, but I didn't love it either. Rape had changed how I experienced it. My body was a reminder of what had happened, and for years I did not treat it well. I gained forty pounds eating fast food and ice cream as my main sources of nutrition. I didn't exercise very much, if at all. I was in a constant state of stress, anxiety and panic. Sometimes my feelings became full-blown manifestations, other times they were quiet, invisible knots in my stomach that kept me from thinking clearly, acting confidently, and healing.

My body also had its own reaction to rape. I developed high blood pressure, which I still have today. The diagnosis came while I was in school for my master's degree, post-meltdown in front of the judge. I don't remember not feeling well, but I went to the student health center to make an appointment with one of the campus therapists. I decided to take advantage of the basic medical check-up offered in the clinic. My blood pressure that day was 200/100. From the looks the doctor and nurse gave each other, I understood the severity of the situation. They prescribed medication and asked me to come back every day for the next two weeks to have my pressure checked.

It's critical to pay attention to the signals your body sends you. If you don't know, normal blood pressure is 120/80. Heart disease is the number one killer of women in the United States. Number one. It is called the "silent killer" because women go for years without feeling any kind of unusual, dramatic symptoms. According the Centers for Disease Control (CDC), more deaths in women result from heart disease than breast cancer. I knew that this condition was common in my family, so I was not totally surprised when the clinic gave me my results. It would take several years before the connection between my health and my trauma would become clear.

During a visit to a holistic doctor, I was shocked to hear her explain how high blood pressure is often connected to pent up rage or anger. She said that my illness was a manifestation of my repression of deep-seated feelings resulting from that experience. In reality, it was probably a whole lot of other things too, with the final doozy acting as the catalyst to a lifelong relationship with blood pressure medications.

Power over my body is something I thought I had lost.

High blood pressure signaled the need to take care of my body and focus on healing it. I wasn't quite sure how I was going to do that because I wasn't looking (or ready for) self-defense classes, or any kind of martial arts. It needed to be more simple and softer than that. I needed to dig deep and reconnect with my physicality in way that was not built on conflict and combat. I needed to find my connection to the basic essence of my body.

I gradually took back power, first through walking, and then by running. This activity helped me in so many ways! First, there was the act/ritual of going outside. Specifically by myself, though walking with friends also brought great joy to me. I walked on the streets of my neighborhood and in nearby parks. Just being outside brought me peace—hearing myself breathe, listening to the sounds of nature, and feeling life happening around me helped restore something inside that had been shut away. My mind processed, wandered, and mused as my feet and legs carried me forward. When I was ready, I would begin to run and push my body out of its comfort zone to find strength and power. I hurt in a lot of places and I wasn't always so disciplined.

There were runs where I cried for miles, and not just tears-streaming-down-my-face crying, but that kind of deep, primal crying that took my breath away. It was my chance to release all the emotions that I had compacted into tight knots deep in the fibers of my body. I felt cleansed after each outing—and I lost a few pounds too. Good for my soul and my body.
There were other paths toward physical healing. I began

to seek out the mind/body connection with a deeper intention. I have received care and guidance from several holistic doctors who practiced different methodologies to treat a whole range of human conditions. Focuses on food, energy work like Reiki, herbal remedies, meditation and so many other modalities served as guides on the path of release and renewal. This was a beautifully hard time of learning how to care for myself, and of recognizing the responsibility I had in my own healing. There is no magic cure for the invisible traces of grief, pain, rage and unworthiness that the experience of rape left in my body.

Despite the steps forward, I have found there is no straight road that leads back to myself. The journey to reconnect and learn to love my body again continues on and on. My sense of femininity had been injured, badly. I couldn't look at my body and didn't want anyone else to see it either. You can imagine the wonders it did for my love life—not! My surface interaction with the world became tough and intolerable. Even as I pushed myself physically, I was aloof to most of those around me. There was an invisible boundary, moat, ocean that very few people and loves ever got past. My internal barriers helped me cover my pain and shame, but I didn't stop there. To truly complete my defenses, I needed armor. This is where the coats came in.

I spent more money than anyone living in Los Angeles ever should on coats. I covered up as much as possible for someone living in a city of eternal summer. I bought vintage coats, mostly. I love their beautiful details—the buttons, the collars, the fabrics and stitching. Most of all, I loved their survival. I didn't know their history, but I found my way to them and sensed a connection with these pieces of slightly worn and damaged clothing. They had managed to remain beautiful and worthy of a second life, despite it all. I didn't understand why I was so drawn to coats until my BFF intervened. We were in a vintage shop, and I was heading to the check-out counter with a coat in hand.

"Girl, do you really need another coat? What is really going on?" she asked.

And just like that, it came together in my mind. I wanted to be covered up and protected, but there was a part of me that longed to feel beautiful, too. Clothes were at once a battlefield and a protector (I'm not even going to get into makeup). I wanted to look good and I wanted to cover myself up—so that no one could see my pain or hurt me again. Slowly, with the help of my loved ones, I began to shift and feel confident with wearing bright colors, dresses and skirts, slightly lower necklines, and even Prince-purple metallic leggings in public! Slowly, I began to feel pretty and safe in clothes, and in my imperfect, curvy body.

A childhood passion also opened another way to reconnect with my physical being: dancing. I love to dance. There isn't a style of music or dance that I would not like to try. It gets underneath my skin, in my bones and deep into my soul. It is language that needs no words, one that brings instant joy and connection. I've taken classes on and off and gone to many parties to dance all night. I've had dance sessions in my living room and just about anywhere else where there was music that moved me. My mom liked to tell the story of watching me through the rearview mirror as a I wiggled about in my car seat to whatever was playing on the radio. Little did I know that this outlet would become such an important part of my healing journey so many years later.

And then there is the sex part of this story. As I type these words, I feel all kinds of discomfort in my physical body, from tears (which I am masterfully holding back), a knot in the pit of my stomach, to fidgeting. My mind is quickly trying to find excuses not to include this section. Deep breath. Another one. Another one. Ok.

I wasn't in love with my body, so I wasn't fully conscious, thoughtful or intentional about how I shared it, especially with my romantic partners. Sex became my weapon of choice in the years following that night. I participated without emotion. It was functional. I did not seek a connection, not even to my own body. It was a way to control the men who came into my life. Physical intimacy should not be a weapon. But it was the only way I could go there without reliving my own rape experience. If I denied the value and power of sex, I could reign in my own feelings of powerlessness and unworthiness.

Sex became a way to hurt men. Oh, the irony of that statement. I admit it was not a good time for me, but I was trying to heal and be a "normal" human being again. I was surviving. I did have a breakthrough one day. It was not pretty, and I am eternally grateful to have had encountered someone strong enough to understand and to allow this catharsis. I am aware of the value, the true beauty and gift of physical intimacy.

That's it. That's all I can write about this right now.

ON THE ROCKY ROAD
(Unfortunately not ice cream) of self-love when falling in love.

This has probably been the most challenging part of my healing journey—vulnerability. Especially being vulnerable with someone who enters my life with the intention to love me. The walls I built with tears, shame, guilt and fear after I was raped were solid. I think my past loves would tell you how draining it was to continually encounter and push against my blockades. I can see this side of the story very clearly now, too. Because I was also tired and drained from trying to wrestle the legion of mini-monsters in my head that were keeping me from being the person of love whom I was meant to be. It was a battle on two fronts, and there were no winners.

What my brain did to protect me, to keep me from feeling that deep pain, meant also keeping out all of the good feelings that life presented. I could give love to everyone else but, in my mind, I wasn't worthy of it. This is the truth of it: I felt tainted and could not receive love.

This time of self-imposed disconnection has also been a lovely (not!) look into who I am and how closely I was aligning my value as a person with the value of the rape experience. An unfair comparison to be sure! And W-R-O-N-G, wrong! What happened to us was not our fault. It wasn't, isn't and that's that! (Ok enough preaching, but this is my story and I get to say what I want!)

So, what did I do to get through this? I fumbled and stumbled through it! There was no other way. I sought out therapy, I learned Buddhist philosophy and meditation, I attended spiritual retreats where I heard some beautiful

Buddhist Lamas and Toltec shamans, I prayed to the Virgen de Guadalupe, our Lady of Fatima, and St. Maria Gorretti (patron saint of rape victims). I sat quietly in nature to breathe in its cleansing beauty.

There are so many beliefs, methods, and spiritual practices to draw strength from, and there is no particular way to go about doing so. The negativity I moved away from were the things—and people, not going to lie—that were judgmental. I was doing enough of that on my own. I benefited most from human beings like myself, who had survived tremendous tragedies and still walked around with love in their hearts and joy on their faces. These were my role models. They became the teachers on the road back to loving myself unconditionally. I aimed for the sort of love a boy-crazy quiceañeara who gives her heart freely might feel—only this time, directing that kind of powerful joy toward myself.

I admit, I am still healing. These wounds are deep. But ... I have loved equally deeply, I have laughed so hard my stomach hurt, and I have felt the kind of contentment that only comes from believing tomorrow will bring more happiness my way. Thank goodness for a beautiful circle of friends and lovers who remind me of who I am, and who push me outside of my self-imposed confinement.

ON THE ROADS THAT LED TO INVISIBLE TRIGGERS
That made me feel like a psychopath.

There have been times in my healing journey where I have been surprised by the explosion of triggers I thought I had quieted (erased, annihilated, stomped on, trashed) through various healing modalities and the passing of time. I haven't always been able to pinpoint the exact trigger, but there have been times when my fight or flight reflex definitely kicked into high gear. The men with me had no idea what was happening in that moment. And not all were innocent, either. This isn't a blame game. Certain behaviors of their own choosing connected me back to a memory where I wasn't safe, protected, or able to stop the situation.

If you could see me now, I am shaking my head and blushing because what followed in these moments was the adult version of having a full out tantrum in the middle of a crowded supermarket. Tears, yells, kicks and all. It may seem irrational, but really, these are natural responses when a need hasn't been met, or in reaction to unshakable feelings of danger.

My reactions have happened during some awkward times—like when I am on a second or third date, and suddenly, out of nowhere, I have a meltdown and start to cry uncontrollably. Not loud or dramatic, telenovela-style, but silent tears that slowly start to make their way down my face into my food, drink, and napkin. Awkward! Often, they lead to a conversation I was not intending to have, and to feeling like an out-of-control drama queen.

I've talked to a lot of people about these instances, trying find understanding as I hear myself repeating details. I have a lot of theories and should probably seek out a professional to help me put things in place—and then move on! And yet, there is a vague notion of comfort and protection in these reflexes because they are familiar. They remind me of how far I have come and how the deep areas of mind and body still hold this memory.

These moments are opportunities to acknowledge and course-correct. Each time, that correction happens a little bit faster. That, my friends, is called healing! I extend my apologies to the souls who have been on the receiving end of my meltdown, and my deep gratitude to those amazing beings who have responded with love and kindness after intimately witnessing my pain, first-hand.

The journey to self-acceptance is a rocky road. Getting there, to self-love, is divine. I am still on my way.

ON BELIEVING MY SMILE
My favorite accessory, and how it went from plastic to solid gold.

I mastered the art of "OK,", "I am fine," and "everything is great" in those years after rape. Unbreakable, strong, determined, empty. Empty, scared and alone. I was raised by a very strong Mexican mother (thank goodness!), whose beautiful smile was like a magical potion of love. She taught my sister and me to be problem-solvers, to make the best of things and situations. I mention this because I inherited her smile. The same smile that became my way to hide from the truth, from self-acceptance, from forgiveness, from healing.

This automatic facial reflex kept me from having to deal with my new reality. I look at pictures from those years and I look funny to me. I'm caught somewhere between fake smile and sadness. If observed really closely, there is sadness in my eyes in almost every single photograph. I couldn't be authentic because I did not, and could not, speak my truth. I was ashamed that it had happened to me—a good, smart, catholic school girl with high expectations. A kind, strong, independent girl, who is proud of being her mother's first-born daughter. How could this have happened? How could I have let this happen? These, and many other questions like these, led to years of sadness and self-judgment.

The first step—and the only real way to start the real healing in your life—is this: BELIEVE yourself! Believe yourself! Believe yourself! In spite of all the self-doubt, in spite of what noise comes back at you, in spite of who this person is in the hierarchy of your family relations. Believe in the validity of your intuition, your feelings, and your body's physical reactions (tears, anxiety, stomach aches, panic, vomiting, uncontrollable shaking—I felt all of these at some point during my healing, even though the person in this incident was not related to me or part of my family circles).

Family and framily (friends that feel like family) were crucial to healing. They hold the keys to the pieces of you that you might have lost in those moments (or years) that robbed you of your body, soul and spirit. The conversations aren't easy, especially if you have experienced this as a younger person. The revelations about having an experience like this to tell will change your relationships. Depending on the details of your experience, you might see your conversation blow up in your face—especially if your situation is tied to someone in your family's circle. Unfortunately, this reaction is commonly experienced by a lot of women in our Latino communities. Luckily for me, I had my sister. I talked a lot with her, and she was there to remind me of what I was like before, to remind me that this wasn't my fault and to pull me out of the dark hole I'd climb into now and then. She was a lifeline.

Family and framily played a critical role in uncovering my real smile because their care, concern and love helped me begin to feel secure again. And when I started to hold my own private pity parties, they came in to shut it down (like the police did at a lot of the house parties I went to in East LA). Non-judgmental support was what I received. Unconditional love was what I felt. Renewed optimism, strength and the feeling that I was protected helped turn that squiggly line of confusion back into the smile my mother bequeathed me through her DNA.

ON BEING FUN AGAIN
Because really, I had no energy for that.

I wasn't fun. I poked holes at anyone's joy with tales of fear, risk, and paranoia. I tried. I wanted to be fun, but I just couldn't let go. There was this sensation in my body, like a fire alarm, warning me that if I broke through to the fun side I would somehow be putting myself in danger. Pretty crazy, right? But it's true. In my wounded mind, being fun, happy-go-lucky, and adventurous made me vulnerable to rape. It was a dark and unavoidable part of finding my smile again. Separate, but related, to my journey of finding the confidence to be fully present, alive and joyful.

ON LIFE TODAY, MY FAVORITE LOVE STORY.

In this time of #MeToo, of political dissonance, of the growing strength of women's voices and power, I feel hopeful and at peace. There are some days that are not so great, but I have learned that every day brings a new opportunity to begin again, to learn something new, to let go of something that no longer serves me. This life brings all kinds of experiences, some requiring more effort and strength than we thought we ever had. I have decided to be happy, no matter what. I leave you with these final worlds: love yourself, deeply. You are not alone. So many of us are around you, waiting to support you no matter where you are in your journey.

If you think you hear distance in some of my story, you do. You are not imagining it. I have intentionally decided to create distance between my rape experience then and my life experience now. Yes, it is part of my personal history—and yes, it has forever affected how I see and interact with the world. But it is not the only thing I have experienced. There have been so many wonderful things that I have seen and felt.

I was in the delivery room when my niece was born, and her sweet little cry was the best thing I have ever heard. I spent the night sleeping in a beautiful tent with two of my favorite people, and then witnessed a sunrise in the Sahara Desert. I got to walk down into the base beneath the Sun Pyramid in Teotihuacán and sit in complete darkness in the same spot where elders, centuries before, prayed before making the decision to build on this site. I visited my grandmother's hometown of Batopilas and then stayed with the Rarámuri in Chihuahua alongside a group of strangers who became lifelong friends. I have had amazing conversations with my sister without speaking a single word. I performed as a belly dancer a few times and didn't fall, trip or injure myself—and my mom got to witness it! I've run half marathons, and I didn't even start running until I turned 40. So many wonderful things and people! My heart is full, and I look forward to living peacefully and in love.

Finally, this is a love story, my love story. The real kind of love story. The one you build because you want a better world. The one you keep rebuilding even though it will fall apart every once in a while, because life is a wild ride of a lot of things. It is a love story you can only have with yourself. Love yourself deeply, you will never regret it.

"Be a lamp, or a lifeboat, or a ladder. Help someone's soul heal."

Rumi

JENNIE ESTRADA
Indigenous Elder, Reiki Master and Energy Healer

I, Sister Weeping Willow decend from a matrilineage of Yaqui healers. Los Angeles is my birthplace. I honor my Mexican-American and Yaqui roots. Retired from corporate America, I followed my passion for working with people's bodies and hearts. My medicine is Reiki and Energy Healing. I've become stronger and have grown on my healing journey.

I am a co-founder of the Yo También Healing Movement, a Reiki Master, and a Certified Massage Therapist and Esthetician. As council member of Native American Concerns of the Archdiocese of Los Angeles, I was involved in healing relations between Native Americans and Catholicism.

As an Indigenous elder, maintaining my traditions is essential to Keeping the Wisdom of my Ancestors ALIVE.

BELIEVING MATTERS

My story is both a story and a heartfelt appeal to care for those around us, especially the children and young people in our lives. Watching someone go through the pain of sexual trauma changes you profoundly. Sometimes it's the slightest change in their behavior, or it's just a gut feeling you get. Whatever this feeling is, don't be afraid to ask that question. Are you all right and are you safe? **Remember: Believing Matters**. This chapter is my story about being an observer and about becoming an advocate. I hope to share...

I met my future godchild when she was 5 years old, and I was visiting her parents in Northern California. The first time I laid eyes on her, she was standing behind her mother's legs looking up at me with a sad shyness in her eyes. Whenever I visited she would always make her way to me, and I would wonder why she clung to me so tightly. After many visits, she asked me for my phone number and address and asked if she could call and write to me. I agreed, and she started to call me at least once a week, sometimes more, and she would write letters to me. Over time, we developed a deep, almost mother-daughter relationship. Through the years she and her family came to visit quite often. They would usually stay with me, or at least she stayed with me. We grew very close to each other.

When my goddaughter was about 12 or 13 years old, we had one our weekly phone conversation, and she sounded especially sad and worried. Her parents were away for the weekend, and she was left home with her two older brothers. I knew about this getaway, so I thought nothing of her calling me. However, the more we spoke I knew something was very wrong. I started to worry because I knew her parents were not coming home until early that evening. I kept asking her what was bothering her, but she wouldn't answer. I asked her if she was safe, and she told me she was. I wondered if anyone other than her two brothers were in the house, and she said it was only the three of them. Then I asked if her brothers had harmed her in any way and the answer was no.

Finally, I asked the worst thing I could think of, "Has someone touched or hurt you in any way?" I was confident the answer would be no, but instead, she said, "Yes, a family member has molested me." I thought, "Oh shit, now what do I do? Since I was 400 miles away?" I told her that I would fly up to be with her, but she said she would be okay because her parents would soon be home. I asked her if she wanted to tell me about it. She proceeded to tell me that a close member of her family had been sexually molesting her since she was about 3 or 4 years old. I was enraged, shocked and disgusted, and I was heartbroken for her to have suffered this by herself. After she finished telling me her story, I again told her, I could fly there in an hour, so I could be with her, "I want to be with you when you tell your mom." She said, "No, Nina." I made her promise me that she would tell her mom as soon as she got home. I made the decision to respect her wishes and let her tell her mother alone because I understood culturally this is how it should happen. I knew I needed to give them time to discuss this as mother and daughter. I told her that I would call back in a few hours and if she hadn't informed her mom by then, I would have to tell her mom.

When I hung up the phone, I cried and cried for hours. *How could an adult, let alone a family member, do this to a child?* To my godchild. Then it hit me why she was always so sad. It finally made sense to me. That is the day when all things changed. I felt more responsible for my goddaughter. I called her daily and provided as much support as I could. We wrote letters to each other, and her letters were more insightful than our conversations. She didn't hold back in her letters; she expressed all her feelings and all her hurts.

In spite of our calls and letters, she grew more depressed. It was getting close to her spring break, so I sent for her. We went to my brother's vacation home, which was right across from the ocean, in Laguna Beach. We went there for healing, and it is still our healing place. It will always be ours until we cross over.

I know this experience will never go away from me. I do not have birth children, and she is the closest I'll ever come to having my own daughter. We both believe I am her re-birth mother. That is why I am so broken-hearted about what had happened to her. *How did I not see something was wrong, that something bad was going on?* The way I currently live with this is my understanding that I came into her life after the molestation had already begun and I only knew her as a shy sad child. She could have been unhappy for any number of reasons. I lived in Southern California, so I didn't see her every day. Phone conversations only allowed me to hear what she wanted me to know. These facts do not take away my pain, but they do let me move forward. This experience coincidentally happened as I began my own personal spiritual journey. That journey has helped me to trust my instincts more. It has also allowed me to forgive those family members who have hurt my goddaughter so profoundly. This wasn't easy because I personally know these molesters and enablers. However, I knew that if I didn't forgive them, I couldn't have a relationship with them. I made this choice because it was my goddaughter's choice to forgive. I have honored and respect her decision.

My goddaughter has gone through a lot of pain and disappointment, but this experience hasn't taken away her beautiful spirit because she is a survivor. I respect how she has maneuvered her way through this terrible experience. I truly mean that because she comes from a Latino family where all bad and ugly things are kept a secret. I am so proud of how she has grown into a beautiful woman of substance. She married a wonderful man, has two children, and two grandchildren. This is not to say that life has been a cakewalk for her. She is still processing and forgiving those who have hurt her in the past. But she is a survivor, and she'll be just fine! "Right, Mija? Just Fine."

I am your re-birth mom, and I have written this story with much love and respect.

When the founders of the Yo También Healing Movement first discussed putting together a book of sexual trauma healing experiences, I knew I had to write a story of my non-sexual trauma experience and how **Believing Matters.** You see, I have never personally experienced this horrific act. *Thank you, Creator.* However, as you have read my story I have experienced this with someone I love dearly; my goddaughter.

I have thought long and hard on our Yo También Healing Movement. We are here to help heal those minds, hearts, and bodies who have suffered in silence and out loud. I believe that those who have been traumatized need to be made whole again. When people suffer from any trauma, they need to acknowledge the wound and not let it define them as its victim. It is essential to let the world know they are survivors. Only then can they reclaim their lives.

The members of the Yo También Healing Movement are dedicated to helping heal those who have suffered these sexual traumas, as well as those who have caused this suffering. At this time in our healing movement, we are not here to blame or shame anyone. We are here to honor those survivors and to help those who still feel like victims cross over to the healing.

I would like to say to all those who have chosen to write their stories; I have the utmost respect for you. I will continue to pray for your healing and also for those who have suffered alone by keeping their trauma silent.

The members of the Yo También Healing Movement also want to include those men and women who have caused or helped cause these traumatic sexual acts of violence. Those individuals are broken spirits who also walk amongst us with much pain and shame.

I have also thought about how I can best serve these survivors. I have asked the Creator to allow me to be his healing connection here on Mother Earth. I am a Reiki Master 1 & 2, which means I practice energy healing. I have studied Peruvian Shamanic healing and have access to other Shaman Healers, both female and male. Finally, I am a massage therapist who uses aromatherapy in my Healing practice.

I knew as soon as my co-founders, and I discussed this healing endeavor, I needed to ask my goddaughter if she felt she could participate in our healing book endeavor. I knew this will help in her healing. Please remember that we all have the ability to help those around us who are suffering and healing from sexual trauma.

As a Healer, I have learned to:

1. Listen with all your heart without judgment.
2. Hold sacred space for them. This means to pray either with them or just myself, and to let them know that I believe them.
3. To respect whatever path they choose to take.
4. Remind them that they are not alone.
5. Once you have accepted this journey with them. Be truthful and patient, in the end, only your concern and kindness matters. Aho and Amen

---

"Doing the best at this moment puts you in the best place for the next moment."

Oprah Winfrey

ANITA L. SANCHEZ, PHD
Author, Speaker, Leadership Consultant, Trainer, Inclusion Thought Leader

Anita Sanchez, Ph.D., Aztec and Mexican-American, is an inspiring speaker and international bestselling author of The Four Sacred Gifts: Indigenous Wisdom for Modern Times, and Success University for Women in Business. Anita bridges indigenous wisdom with science to inspire and equip people to enjoy empowered lives and careers. Clients include Fortune 500 companies, education and non-profit organizations. Her diversity and inclusion programs and strategies for creating positive change are benchmarked. Member of the Transformational Leadership Council, board member of the Evolutionary Business Council, Bioneers, and the Pachamama Alliance.

www.AnitaSanchez.onlinepresskit247.com
www.FourSacredGifts.com to download the free song based on her book.

www.SanchezTennis.com

THE FOUR SACRED GIFTS:
PERSONAL AND SPIRITUAL GROWTH AFTER TRAUMA

I saw a post on Instagram recently. It said,

"Pain is inevitable, suffering is optional."

That might have an aspect of truth to it, and, it can trivialize the anguish of carrying the effects of trauma or abuse. Yes, pain may be an opportunity for growth but that doesn't mean this process is easy or straightforward. Nonetheless, these experiences provide building blocks for becoming the people we were meant to be.

We were not meant to live lives without challenge, obstacles or pain. The question is, how can we transform our painful experiences into catalysts for our personal and spiritual growth?

FORGED IN THE FIRE

Trauma is all too present in the human experience. Research reveals that an estimated 70% of adults in the U.S. have experienced trauma, and up to 20% of these develop Post-Traumatic Stress Disorder (PTSD).

The term 'post-traumatic growth' was coined in the 1950s. The University of North Carolina - Charlotte Posttraumatic Growth Research Group define it as "positive change experienced as a result of the struggle with a major life crisis or a traumatic event".

The concept, however, is as old as humankind. The experience of personal growth after trauma is prevalent in wisdom traditions of indigenous people, and the religions of many cultures. It can, as well, be found in literature and philosophy.

It is important to understand, though, that these wisdom traditions about growth after trauma are not talking about the traumatic event itself. They refer instead to how the traumatic event can be the catalyst for positive change. Post-traumatic growth is the process that begins after the traumatic event.

Which brings us back to the question: how can we transform our painful experiences into catalysts for our personal and spiritual growth?
I know that it is possible for each of us to rise from the ashes of your trauma like a phoenix and soar higher than we ever dared dream. I will share with you my story and how the four sacred gifts led the way for me.

A TRILOGY OF TRAUMA

It was a hot, humid mid-summer afternoon in 1967. My mom, my younger brother, sister, and I were in the kitchen having a tall glass of iced cold Kool-Aid. There was a knock on the door and I followed Mom to see who it was. There stood two police officers. I was frightened to see them because when police showed up in our neighborhood, it was usually to arrest someone.

"Are you Mrs. Sanchez, the wife of Phillip Sanchez?" Asked one of the officers.

"Yes," my mom responded.

"Ma'am, may we come in?"

Mom opened the door, quiety nodding them into the living room.

"I'm very sorry to tell you that your husband was in an accident, and he was killed at the scene."

I stood there dazed and I felt my mom lean heavily on me for a moment until she somehow recovered herself. The officers asked if they could sit down and ask a few more questions.

"Mrs. Sanchez, do you know of anyone who would want to hurt your husband? Anyone who would want him dead?"

My throat tightened and my stomach heaved with nausea as a whirl of mixed emotions flooded through my system. Guilt, disbelief, confusion, fear and shame. But also, relief.

Guilt that I had killed my forty-one-year-old father with my thoughts of wanting him to leave, even die, so that the years of sexual abuse would end. Fear that my mom, brothers, sisters, and others, would learn my shameful secret. That from age four to thirteen, I was a participant in my abuse through my silence and resignation that there was no other life for me.

"No, I don't know anyone who would want to kill my husband," my mom replied.

"Mrs. Sanchez it appears that, earlier today, a white man

and a black man had a heated argument in the bar around the corner from here," the policeman said. "Your husband entered the bar several hours later and sat on the stool where earlier the black man had sat while arguing with the white patron. It appears the white man returned to the bar, saw your husband's dark skin and fired two shots. Your husband was pronounced dead at the scene."

HATE SPEAK

A few days after the funeral, there was another knock at the door. We assumed it would be more family members and neighbors bringing food and words of condolences. Mom unlocked the screen door with me behind her. I peeked around Mom's round body and saw a slender, white woman and a young boy about my age, standing on our small wood porch.

The woman introduced themselves as the wife and son of the man who murdered my father. She continued, "I am sorry to bother you, Mrs. Sanchez, but I just had to tell you that my husband is a good man. He would never have killed your husband, if he knew that he was Mexican. My husband thought that he was black." The woman continued to speak, but I couldn't hear her words anymore. Now, she was saying something about black people always causing trouble. Pressed against my mom, I could feel her body become tense and trembling.

My mother's stern voice interrupted the woman, "Stop! Stop! You don't even know what you are saying. You don't even know the kind of hatred you are speaking in front of your son. I want you to know that I will try very hard to pray for you. But, now, please get off of my porch!"

Mom closed the screen door and locked it. She walked back to the kitchen; I could tell that she was quietly crying. I was crying inside, too. I was overwhelmed by everything that was happening and I just wanted my family and me to be left alone. Alone to build a life with love and without fear of being hurt.

Later that evening, mom called all six of us, my brothers and sisters, to our tiny living room. As we gathered to sit on the couch, she pointed to the newspaper clipping with a photo of my father's body in a pool of blood. "I want you kids to know that a white man murdered your father, not the white race. It was one man. The picture you see here in the paper is ugly and disrespectful. The dead and their souls always should be treated with respect. And the dead person's families, you and me, we also deserve respect."

Still pointing at the photo in the newspaper she said, "This is racism. When a violent death or accident happens to a white person, the body is not shown. But when a black person, an Indian, or Mexican is killed, the pictures are right on the front page. I do not want you to hate white people. However, you must watch where you are always, for there are ignorant people who will want to harm you. I believe that most people are not this way. Most people want to be kind, just as I taught you to be."

My brothers, sisters and I all sat quietly with tears in our eyes, taking in what our mother had just said.

KILLING THE PAIN

Several months later, I no longer had to be fearful of my father's violence, drunken anger and sexual abuse. However, I was naïve to think that the horrible images and memories of abuse would stop. In my worst moments, I found myself drowning in memories and feelings of shame, fear and pain. I was thirteen years old and I decided that I could not live this way anymore. On that Missouri afternoon, I resolved to end my life.

Climbing on a chair, I quietly stepped on the yellow Formica kitchen countertop, so I could reach the highest kitchen cabinet where my mother stored her medicine to keep it out of the reach of the children. I grab a large bottle of aspirin and quietly return upstairs to the bedroom I shared with my two sisters. Behind the closed door, I began gulping water to quickly swallow the pills. They stuck in my throat so I drank more water to get them down. I imagined going to sleep and forever ending the horrible images of my dad and me.

It was not, though, my day to die. My body rejected the aspirin and I began to violently throw up; my whole-body convulsing. The sounds of vomiting quickly brought my family to my side. I heard my mother's voice, as if in the distance, saying, "What were you thinking? You are not to die! There has been enough death in this house."

And as I lay there convulsing, I no longer wanted to die. I begged the spirits: 'Oh, please, please, let me get through the pain. I want to live; I am supposed to be here in the circle with my three brothers, my two sisters and my mom.'

For a moment, part of me drifted away from the pain and I sensed the loving touch of my abuela's soft, wrinkled hand as we walked to the green vegetable garden in her backyard. I could feel the warmth of the dark, rich dirt over my hands as she helped me plant a flower seed, a sunflower seed, a mirasol. She lovingly guided me out of the pain, giving me the courage to wake up and be with my family.

INDIGENOUS WISDOM AND VISIONS

Having survived my own trauma, and found the gifts within my experience, I now travel the world sharing indigenous wisdom and positive psychology with people everywhere who are working to heal and grow themselves, their businesses, their communities, and the planet.

I know, for sure, that we each have the potential, and the tools, to open to a new experience of personal growth.

On my journey, I had to stop running away from the hurt, mistreatment and trauma. I had to go through intense reflection to deal with overwhelming feelings of loss, anger and emotional pain. As whole human beings, we are not meant to stop there. We are not meant to remain in constant reflection about the hurt and intense mistreatment. For growth to occur, I had to let go and let in opportunities for change and evolution. I had to open myself to the many supports that I have received, and continue to receive, from people, animals, nature and spirit.

I know I am not alone in this. I feel great compassion for the pain and suffering endured by you and your loved ones. It's possible to move through this, though. I want you to know that by moving through your trauma, and evolving as a result of it, you can have:

- new opportunities and possibilities in your life,
- positive change in your relationships with others,
- an increased sense of confidence and personal strength,
- expanding appreciation for life, and/or
- deepening of joy and spiritual life.

My healing, and thriving, have been guided by four sacred gifts that were received from Spirit by my indigenous elders and then offered to all humanity. These four gifts are intended to usher in a new season of humanity and I have written about them at length in my book, The Four Sacred Gifts – Indigenous Wisdom for Modern Times (Simon and Schuster).

The sacred work of the four gifts was begun at a gathering in 1994 at Turtle Mountain Chippewa of indigenous elders, healers and leaders from the four directions – including the Americas, Asia, the Arctic and Africa. This gathering marked the beginning of a new era because it is now time for all the human family to come together as one – red, black, white and yellow.

During that weekend at Turtle Mountain Chippewa, the 27 Elders spoke their own languages, prayed their prayers, meditated, sang and danced. They built a hoop out of a tree branch, tying one hundred eagle feathers onto it. The hoop is an evolving symbol of humanity.

Spirit guided them to then place four sacred gifts, four powers, into the hoop necessary for us all to receive in order to do the sacred work before us of remembering our oneness.

Spirit said to the Elders, "Take it to the people for it is not yours; it belongs to all the human family – red, black, white and yellow."

These sacred gifts are intended to help us remember how to be in harmony and balance with ourselves, people and the earth. They have been a big part of my own journey of healing, growth and joy. I use these gifts every day, trusting their centering power within myself. Now, I invite you to receive them into your own heart. Take the four gifts to support you in being a whole human who knows how to be in 'right relationship' with yourself, other people, earth and spirit. The Four Sacred Gifts are as follows:

The Power to Forgive the Unforgiveable
This gift enables you to free yourself from the burden of carrying hurts and mistreatments.

The Power of Unity
This gift enables you to reconnect with who you really are, with the world, with Spirit.

The Power of Healing
This gift enables you to heal yourself and support the healing of others.

The Power of Hope
This gift enables you to create a positive new life, the life of your dreams.

THE GIFT OF FORGIVEABLE THE UNFORGIVEABLE

This is the sacred gift that will finally release you from past pain and trauma. Whether it be offering forgiveness to yourself or others, though, it can be the hardest step to take.

Without forgiveness we can become trapped in a cycle of recommitting to our pain, instead of releasing ourselves from the pain.

If forgiveness were easy, we'd all be doing it more often. So why is forgiving the unforgivable a gift? Forgiving the unforgivable is a path to true freedom. Forgiveness does not mean forgetting the hurt or mistreatment, it does not mean lack of confidence, or disloyalty to yourself, your tribe, family, or group. Forgiveness is not about condoning hurtful actions nor is it about not seeking justice; it is about allowing yourself to live free from the burden of continuing to carry pain and anger inside you.

In forgiving, we are releasing ourselves from the prison of what did, or did not happen, or what we wished had happened. Through forgiveness, we show true self-love. We can choose to use our energy to be present to what is now unfolding. When you use this gift, you are no longer locked in the chains of righteous pain and hurt – or the insidious illusion that these pains and hurts are our identity; what define us.

The Elders teach us that forgiveness is a spiritual practice.

Rather than resort to violence, either physical or emotional, to control or exert power over someone or something that hurt us, we can choose harmonious connection. This spiritual practice grounds us in the awareness that we are part of something larger as we walk our higher spiritual path of letting go and forgiving the unforgivable.

THE PRACTICE OF FORGIVING

How do you do use this gift in your own life? For a start, do not feel you need to forgive the 'big' stuff straight away. Build up to it. Start with the small stuff.

In practicing this gift of forgiveness for myself, I started with lesser hurts. The little wounds that seem easier to forgive. It is a powerful thing, though, when you forgive a trauma in one part of your life, it makes it more possible to forgive a different hurt in another part of your life. With practice and over time, I built up the self-love to free myself from the shame of nine years of being abused as a child.

My father was murdered when I was thirteen years old. I learned that death does not end a relationship; it just made it a bit more complicated to resolve. Fortunately, my mother was still alive so, when I reached the age of 21, I confronted her with my pain from abuse at the hands of my father - her husband. As well as my pain from her neglect. The courage to confront the trauma with my mother was key to releasing that trauma. I was able to create a new, loving relationship with my mother, who also wanted to create a new healthy relationship with me. I gained a growing sense of the joy of being free and discovered new possibilities for vital relationships with others and myself.

As for my father, it is tragic that he lost his life at the young age of 41. It would have been wonderful if he could have reconciled his life and atoned for his abuse. I don't know that he would have chosen that, regardless, I forgive him, and I forgive myself. I am free to live my journey.

The purpose of alchemy was to 'transmute' something lesser to its greatest version; to exoteric, meaning the transmutation of lead into gold, and to esoteric, meaning transforming the alchemist themselves into transcendent, enlightened beings.

Forgiveness, then, becomes an empowering act of spiritual alchemy; a powerful medicine that transforms our hurt and trauma into a catalyst for deeper compassion with oneself and others in the hoop of life. We shift from *'This pain defines me' to 'I choose to be free'*.

Forgiveness frees us to experience joy.
What and who will you forgive?

THE GIFT OF THE POWER OF UNITY

As someone who experienced long-term sexual and racial violence, I swore as a teen that I would never give anyone the chance to hurt me like that again. Being the target of racism, sexism and sexual violence is intensely personal and insidious. So, I built imaginary body armor to keep out the bad stuff. I came to believe that the pain and suffering I endured was my identity. It became part of who I thought I was. I would explain to others that my deep well of pain was so much larger than my tiny well of joy.

This, though, I eventually realized, was a lie, for I did know joy. My 'illusion of separateness body armor' was trying to protect me but over time, I understood that this body armor was imprisoning me. It may have kept out the bad stuff but it was also blocking the good stuff. In the process of pulling this armor firmly around me, I repelled the good things, the life-giving things. Eventually, I realized that wearing this armor was heavy lifting. It took a huge amount of my energy to stay separate from other people and nature. The cost of separation, disunity, from myself and from others was slowly killing me. I began to look about me, seeing how the cost of dis-unity resulted in depression, crime, drug, alcohol and food addiction, suicide, physical and mental abuse, destruction of the natural world, extinction of species, and a general collective despair in individuals and in whole communities.

It is in remembering my connection to my own body, to nature, animals and people that I began to trust that I am part of the Hoop of Life. I am never separate from the Hoop of Life.

UNION WITH NATURE AND PEOPLE

One of the best ways to reconnect to yourself and your body is through nature. *Mi abuelita Azteca* (my little Aztecan grandmother) was the primary source of the indigenous wisdom in my family. I have a dear memory of being five-years-old, standing in her backyard with my sisters, Paula and Olivia. Grandmother Medina had woken us up early that August weekend morning; we stood out by her garden. She had the three of us gather near her sunflower plants as the sun started to rise. It felt magical in her garden. Every hour until darkness returned that night, she had us go back to the sunflower and stand facing the direction the flower was facing. The flower was following the sunlight.

There was so much I learned from being with the sunflower on its journey through the day: even in the darkness, the sunflower stood ready to face the light for another day.

My grandmother helped me understand my connection to all things with this lesson. Getting stuck in my trauma as a teen almost had me forget the truth that I wasn't alone. Nature is always here – trees, sun, birds, water, earth, grass. I am a part of nature, and nature is a part of me. We are part of the sacred; everyone is part of the sacred. Yes, that is what my grandmother and other elders had taught me.

This doesn't mean that everyone is behaving in a sacred way. It doesn't mean we walk away and allow others to abuse us, nor accept all the needless suffering and pain in the world. Instead, this simple truth invites us to really experience our oneness whenever we can – even if it's just for a few moments each day. The more we connect with our oneness, the more our experience of connection begins to grow.

Years later, walking through the pine trees and flower gardens of the University of Colorado campus, I began to remember the feeling of breathing from the top of my head to the tips of my toes and moving my face toward the sunlight. I slowly began to put down my illusion-of-separateness armor to be with nature. It wasn't long that I began to attract professors, administrators and other students who wanted to be true friends, who acknowledged my brightness and who treated me with dignity. As I re-awakened to my connection to life, I began to grow. I began to accept the life-giving connections to others and the beauty within and around me.

It turned out that once I opened myself to the possibility of being a member of a caring, supportive community, I could begin to imagine letting go of that heavy armor. With that recognition of my unity with others, I began to soar!

Joining two friends in an election campaign, I became the first Hispanic and Indigenous woman student body president at the University. The sense of connection I had meant there was no question that I would continue to learn, to grow and to tackle new challenges in getting my master's degree and doctoral degree. Then, my first job allowed me to create the first child abuse prevention day care center in my community. Building on my confidence and experience as a leader in that job, I created my own consulting and training firm and found myself training people in visionary leadership and appreciation of cultural differences and similarities. My sense of unity with others created a whole new path for my life, one dedicated to building life-giving connections for all peoples.

There are still tough days and difficult projects, but I am supported by my celebration of my connection to all of life – people, earth, and spirit every day. I rise above the illusion that we are separate, that our thoughts and actions and ways of being don't affect all of existence.

In realizing our intrinsic connection, we can begin to harness our personal and global power to effect meaningful change. This is the sacred gift of unity. It supports us in having an ever-growing and vital connection with all beings. This is a time when we are called to become and remain united and steadfast —to protect our water, to protect our Mother Earth, and repair the world from the misuse of power and greed.

When we choose to stand in the circle of unity, there is strength. When we understand our interconnectedness, we can transform the world; we can right injustices and restore the dignity of the sacred circle — people, earth, and spirit — by uniting.

This union starts though, with ourselves. It starts with collaboration between one's own heart and mind. Working together instead of pulling in different directions. It requires each of us to embody more of our Higher Selves in this world.

Your Higher Self is more than your five senses. It is the part of you that understands we are part of a universal consciousness that some call God, Allah, Buddha, Nature, Universal energy, Source and more.

As my indigenous elders of Hispanic and other backgrounds share, 'Your Higher Self is the real you, the soul consciousness that is so, so much more than the physical form you know so well. Your Higher Self is the you that is unlimited and eternal, that excites you with inspiration, guides with intuitions and acknowledges the great mystery.'

How can we begin this process of unity within ourselves? Especially when it feels like we are drowning in a world of disunity and distrust in in politics, economics, social and environmental actions?

One of the first steps is empathy and service. be in service to others, volunteering to support people, animals, nature or another favorite cause brings us joy and a sense of loving connection. It is a royal road to moving from victim to thriving. Imagine yourself in the other's place, seeing through their eyes and holding them in the most positive possible light. To Together, we can co-create a just and sustainable world for all of us.

How will you choose connection and union in your life?

THE GIFT OF THE POWER OF HEALING

'Healing' is a term that encompasses many different things. From a song to a person's touch, a poem, a yoga pose, sitting in a community talking circle where you are not judged, being in nature, dance, chanting, meditation, prayer, or a meal prepared with love. All of these, and more, can be healing.

I have found it helpful to understand the idea and practice of 'good medicine' and 'bad medicine'. Good medicine is anyone or anything that aligns us at the spiritual, emotional, mental and physical levels. By contrast, bad medicine is anyone or anything that creates separation or discord between one's spiritual, emotional, mental and physical being. By focusing on good medicine, each of us have the capacity to heal and to support others in their healing process.

To heal my wounds and remove my scars from sexual abuse, I drew on both indigenous wisdom and western medicine. I visited a psychologist and I used anti-depressants when I was suffering from post-partum depression. I am grateful to have access to western medicine. In addition, I drew heavily on indigenous wisdom traditions, including talking circles, sweat lodges, pow wows and other ceremonies.

In drawing on indigenous practices, I found there to be four basic elements of healing: listening; supportive relationships; unconditional love, and a commitment to creative, positive action. As I practiced, practiced and practiced these four elements, I experienced post-traumatic growth. With this practice, my world continues to blossom and expand with new possibilities.

1. LISTENING: One of the essential elements of supporting healing in ourselves and in others is the art of listening. I remember the first time I was taught to listen to a bird, a tree, to an Elder. I was told to listen with the softest part of my ear and the deepest part of my heart. Little did I know that this type of listening would allow me to know when I was no longer in touch with myself. When I no longer was listening to my own body and my spirit, I found myself in the depths of my pain, continually cycling downward in my mind and emotions. When I drew on indigenous healing practices, I was able to bring in the knowledge from my body and the wisdom from my spirit that allowed me to deal with my mind and emotions. As an example, here is a simple breathing practice that I use every day.

Focus on breathing; imagine inhaling from your heart and exhaling from your heart. Inhaling love and kindness and exhaling love and kindness.

2. QUIET YOUR MIND: allow your thoughts to drift away like clouds, let the inner conversation and chatter slow down or even cease. Just keep doing #1.

3. STAY SILENT: let go of your need to say or do anything other than inhaling and exhaling love and kindness. Be present to yourself.

Repeat steps 1-3 as needed to stay present.

When we listen to ourselves, it is possible to identify what needs to be healed and what wants to be created. It is with this listening process of healing that I realized that I was never alone.

SUPPORTIVE RELATIONSHIPS: When I was younger, it was easier to feel that connection with nature and other people. As the pain of abuse grew within me, though, I grew an over-developed sense of danger. It caused me to close myself off from accepting the healing support that was available to me. I now know that I could not have healed on my own. Nature, pets, teachers, co-workers, fellow students and caring family members provided the witness and cheering crowd for me to heal from my early years of violence and set free my desire to learn, grow and create.

Perhaps some of the most supportive relationships that I made were from my volunteering in causes that were important to me. In focusing on service to others, I was able to get some time off from a total focus on my own hurts and sufferings. Being around people who truly cared and gave freely their gifts inspired me to be free to give share my contributions. It was with a desire to serve that I began to open up to and trust supportive relationships.

UNCONDITIONAL LOVE: It is funny how the third element of healing, which is unconditional love, grew from thinking that unconditional love was something you gave to someone else. A person gives unconditional love to a baby, or a small animal, or to the earth that supports us. From the supportive relationships that grew for me, I began to listen to myself and to hear the desire to unconditionally love myself. Taking care of myself, my spiritual, emotional, mental and physical needs was essential. Using this powerful healing element of unconditional love on myself began to erode the limiting belief that I was somehow not worthy of dignity and of unconditional love.

Creative Positive Action: As I watched others care for themselves, I, too, began taking creative positive action in my self-care, my self-love.

One of the self-love practices that lifted me, and remains vital to my health today, is to ask my ancestors, nature, angels or spirit guides each night, before I go to sleep, to provide me with their wisdom and safety. I express my gratitude to all living, seen and unseen beings, that provided me with support and love today including the water, the grocery store clerk, my healthy body, and more. Sometimes the list is long, and I drift to peaceful sleep as I count them off.

Committing to creative positive action is a daily practice. It is a person's decision to live their life, and to tell their story, with a laser-focus on owning the choices that one makes. I choose to apply listening, supportive relationships, and unconditional love to myself and to others. I know that I am human, so there will be times when old hurts and traumas will get triggered, emotions may get stuck in my mind, and I may forget my commitment to be good medicine to myself and to others. However, I have the skills, knowledge and commitment to get into positive action on behalf of myself and on behalf of my relationships with others, people and the earth.

The cycle of healing is a gift that is meant to be used over and over again. My well of joy is so huge in comparison to the small well of pain. I have the resilience and the love to create joy for myself and others, and to do my part to end needless suffering.

What in your life is calling to be healed?

THE GIFT OF THE POWER OF HOPE IN ACTION

Hope is something real. It is an eternal energy source that we can tap into to generate the stamina we need to keep moving toward our vision and dreams.
Every morning we can look up at the morning star, which is the planet Venus, or look at the sunrise and know that it is a new day. We know, deep inside, that hope is an

energy source, an inner certainty that there is something bigger than any one of us. For everyone, hope is a gift of the connection between people, earth, and spirit.

The biggest danger to hope, to imagining something better for our lives, is doubt. Fear of uncertainty, risk, or possible failure, the sense of being not enough and unworthy of a better life, is a killer of the drive to create positive change. Doubt dashes the desire for something new, even when what you currently have is not healthy or life-giving. If you begin feeling paralyzed and unable to make needed change, this is when it is important to practice any one, or all, of the four gifts. Committing to hope, in action, counters the danger of doubt that can grow out of our trauma. We are more than that, and committing to a brighter future is the key to a new and thriving life.

By opening ourselves to hope, we can release the pressure and desire to know everything, the need to think we are in control. It is, in fact, impossible to know all the answers. Any control we think we have is an illusion. Hope, though, is an infinite energy source. It can inspire us and can help pull us through even the most difficult times, as they arise in our lives. Hope ignites our capacity to dream and envision a better reality, and then impels us into positive action. When we have hope, we are triumphant over the pain of the past.

I am filled with hope in co-creating this book with others who have dealt with the violence of harassment and sexual abuse but who refuse to let it be their identity. It is a huge shift to be able to name this violent assault on our humanity. It is a choice to reclaim our power and choose to grow and thrive rather than remain stuck in the pain.

Living these four sacred gifts, daily, creates healthy connection to yourself and others.

What hopes and dreams will you allow to manifest?

COMING FULL CIRCLE

From my own early lessons in oneness and unity, and the painful trials I have been through, I have come to know that I am one with the sacred tapestry of life. I am not my pain, I am not a victim of my father's abuse, I am not a victim of my father's murderer. I am worthy of dignity, as all beings are. I use the Four Sacred Gifts to remember how to be in right relation to all beings, myself included.

Mine is a story of resilience and empowerment. I am a voice for forgiveness, unity, healing, and hope. I know and trust my gifts. My intention in sharing parts of my journey is to offer a path for growing and thriving after a trauma and discovering and trusting your gifts.

Yo, También is not the end of our journey; it is a step along the way of a journey to honor our sacredness, our wholeness, our joy as members of the Hoop of Life.

"This is the kind of Friend you are... Without making me realize my soul's anguished history, You slip into my house at night, And while I am sleeping, You silently carry off all my suffering and sordid past In your beautiful hands."

Hafez

ABEL SALAS
Poet and Writer, Community Activist, Editor and Publisher at Brooklyn & Boyle

L.A. journalist/poet Abel Salas has written for The New York Times, Los Angeles Times Magazine, Los Angeles Magazine, LA Weekly, Los Angeles Review of Books and The Austin Chronicle among others. His poetry has appeared in Zyzzyva, Huizache, Beltway Quarterly, and La Jornada (Mexico), as well as the anthologies Poetry of Resistance: Voices for Social Justice (University of Arizona Press, 2016) and The Coiled Serpent: Poets Arising from the Cultural Quakes and Shifts of Los Angeles (Tia Chucha Press, 2016). His debut poetry collection, *Anatomía de Un Decorazonado/ Heartbreak Anatomy 101* is forthcoming on Ponte Las Pilas Press

THE TRUTH IS THAT

Sitting on the ground inside a dark garage, the nine-year-old boy cups the open end of a Butter Krust bread loaf bag over the lower half of his face. Instead of bread slices, the oblong wrapper is filled with gasoline. The translucent copper-tinted liquid fills the bottom quarter of the plastic bag. Small for his age, he rests his elbows on top of his bent knees and his sneakered feet flatly against the asphalt flooring underneath. Manolo—a step-cousin the boy has known for all of a day and half—sits low and cross-legged beside him. Almost 15, the teenager wears a white t-shirt, creased khakis and high-top canvas Chuck Taylor All-Stars. He holds a Ziplock freezer bag about half-full of the same high octane regular unleaded fuel to his face. The gas comes from heavy-duty aluminum container. The rectangular, red and yellow one-gallon gas can is marked with warnings about the flammability of both its liquid and vaporous contents.

A punctured aerosol spray paint can lies on the ground in a corner not far from where Manolo is seated. Vigorous shaking and several attempts to push down on the button nozzle at the top of the can failed to release any of the paint trapped inside. Frustrated, the older boy had hammered a roofing nail into the side of the canister after first demonstrating how he would have sprayed the paint into one section of a neatly folded black bandana pulled from his back pocket. "Gold and silver are the best. Then you fold this part over like this, put it up to your nose and huff it. That way you don't get any paint on your face," Manolo had explained. Oblivious to the white paint seeping from the hole in the can and staining the ground, Manolo, had looked around and discovered the gasoline used to power the lawn mower.

"We can use the gas. I've done it before. We can't use the paño to huff it, though. You need a plastic baggy. Go and find us a couple, yeah?" Manolo had instructed. All of these—the cousin who calls himself "Mano" for short, the plastic bags, the gasoline can, the fumes curling into his nostrils and down his throat, the bandana, the paint spilling onto the ground from an old can—slip away into a blur as a vaporous stupor wraps its tentacles around his consciousness. Huffing slowly from the plastic bread bag, the boy hangs stoically onto the idea that his complicity will cement the approval he seeks from the tough-looking teenager he'd been tagging along with since the day before yesterday.

His uncle Roko—his father's younger brother—had shown up unexpectedly with his wife Carol and Manolo, her son. His father had been genuinely pleased. The boy knew this from the beaming smile his dad had flashed that morning when they stepped through the front door of the home he and his family had recently moved into. The reserved and steely-eyed teenager had hung back warily until his uncle had introduced him. "This is my step-son, Manolo. Come say hello to your Tío Pete and Tía Julia, son," his uncle had said. Stepping forward to shake hands with the boy's father, Manolo had broken his silence to say "Tío," then lowered and lifted his head with a nod that meant respect. "And say hi to your cousins, starting with your primito here," Roko had added. Hearing the uncle Roko say the word for "little cousin," the boy and the teenager had looked at each other and grinned.

When Uncle Roko had mentioned to his wife and stepson that his older brother Pete and of Pete's children once lived on Mark Street near where they themselves still resided, Mano had let down his guard and loosened up. The boy and his newly-met step-cousin were soon off to themselves. He was still a baby when his family had lived in Kinwood, the younger boy explained, so he didn't remember much about Northside Houston. He knew it was where his Abuela Anita, his dad's mom, lived. Carol and his uncle Roko had spoken quietly with the boy's parents on the morning after their first and only night as guests. Earlier, Mano had taught him how to sit on the handle bars and anchor his feet on the front wheel axle bolts of his own bike, while he steered and pedaled them through the neighborhood, the younger happy to point out the cool things and places. Later, the boy's father had let them know it would be okay if Manolo wanted to stay a few days while his step-father Roko and his mother Carol took care of some things at home. By then, he and Mano were palling around like old camaradas. Mano had even let him handle the small but razor-sharp knife he carried. "Be careful with that, peewee," Mano had warned. "It's not for school boys. You could hurt yourself."

...

The truth is that I began learning about mañas (roughly the "nasties" or "playing doctor" possibly derived from mañoso—meaning one with untoward habits or inclinations, or maniaco—a maniac) long before I was abused. My parents, both raised as evangelical Christians during the 1930s and '40s did everything to protect us and provide us with the ability to distinguish right from wrong. Despite their adherence to strict, Bible

Belt codes of morality and conduct, I was introduced to sexual activity, in pantomime, when I was five or six years old. I recall a teen-aged tomboy cousin named Dolores leading me and my cousin Emily to a secluded area near the ramshackle farmhouse in Dewalt, Texas where my maternal grandparents lived.

My grandfather worked as the caretaker of an agricultural property on the southwestern outskirts of Houston. He and 'Buelita had occupied the rough, clapboard house that came with the job for as long as I could remember. It was situated on farmland where cotton and rice and sugarcane were rotated as staples and reached by a dirt road. Getting from a paved, two-lane highway to Grandma's meant driving across a rickety wooden bridge over an irrigation canal. Visits to see 'Buelita and Abuelito were adventures into boggy brush country where we picked wild berries and marveled at the foamy "snake spit" often left in clumps on low-lying berry bushes. Their home, built two feet above earth often muddy from frequent flooding, was always a hive of activity over which my mom's mother held sway. An iron-willed matriarch, 'Buelita Micaela had little patience for slackers, roustabouts or daydreamers.

My mother was one of ten children born to Micaela and Praxedis, my grandparents. Every now and then, one of that original couple's numerous grandchildren came to stay in their rickety but always warm and bustling house. 'Buelita would put up with these occasional boarders as long as they left her marijuana plants—which she grew exclusively as an additive to rubbing alcohol for relief of rheumatoid and arthritis pain—alone and helped around the property with chores. My cousin Dolores, the eldest of the six kids belonging to my aunt Regina and her husband Juan, may have been living temporarily with 'Buelita and Grandpa at the time.

Out of view of the adults on the porch or other cousins in the front yard, Dolores instructed Emily, who was my age, and I to engage in "mañas," or "doing it." Although fully-clothed, Emily and I giggled sheepishly. Dolores, looking at Emily, said, "It's not supposed to be funny. You're not doing it right. You act like he's tickling you." At that, both Emily and I laughed out loud. Dolores motioned adamantly with her finger on lips to hush us. Though we both did as she asked, Dolores could see that we were anxious and that our enthusiasm had dwindled. "That's okay. Stop. Just forget it," Dolores hissed under her breath. She then instructed me to get on top of her after she laid back on the blanket where we all sat, unbuttoned her jeans and lowered them slightly to reveal white underwear. Sensing my trepidation, she ordered me off and said it sounded like my parents were calling me. After that, I understood "nasties" or "mañas" to be awkward, uncomfortable fumblings that made me feel guilty and queasy at the same time.

...

The hallucinations begin shortly after the thick, pungent gasoline fumes swing past his teeth and tongue. He finds himself sitting on a blue square and perceives a red one swirling into place to form the roof of a box-like encasement taking shape around him. On his left, a blue wall comes into focus and is countered by a red one forming on his right. In front of him, another seemingly solid surface perhaps a foot or so from his face shifts from blue to red and then settles slowly into a blue and red checkerboard pattern. Lowering the bag from his face for a moment, he cranes his neck in an effort to look over his shoulder, worried that he will now be trapped. Fear needles its way into his pores and clouds his perception, taunting him with shadows that dance ominously just beyond the box. His throat constricts and, unable to breathe, he lowers the bag even more, trying to remember where he is. Looking at his right forearm, he watches the skin peel away in seven layers, counting them silently to himself until the horrific sight of bone and blood leaves him gasping. To counter the shock, he resorts to an explanation straight from a comic book, "Maybe I have x-ray vision. That's all. It has to be," he whispers to himself.

Turning away from the frightening vision, he sees Mano through the now translucent blue wall on his left. His step-cousin huffs away, head tilted forward, eyes hooded by thick, swollen eyelids. His milky, unfocused eyes reflect a sliver of daylight from outside trickling in at the bottom of the two wide garage doors, giving them an eerie glow. Dizzy and full of dread, the boy stands abruptly and makes his way through the doorway at the rear of the garage that opens onto a small landing at the bottom of a staircase built between the house and the garage. Closing the door behind him until it catches, he leans back against it. The cool wooden surface, painted a pastel green, comforts him, and he breathes deeply until he no longer feels that his legs will buckle under him.

Opposite him, on the other side of the small landing, is a door leading into the bedroom where his parents sleep and the rest of the house. He wants no one to see him this way, so he starts up the stairs, putting his right hand on the wall to steady himself. He can hear his heart pounding as he climbs one step at a time. The stairs lead to the bedroom he shares with an older brother, a high school senior he seldom sees anymore, and an adjoining room, narrower and windowless. Painted in a darker hue, the space had been, until several months before, a makeshift bedroom for his grand-uncle, a legendary horse tamer named Victoriano. It had been the boy's job to empty and wash the removable plastic waste pail from the portable commode next to the rollaway cot where the rugged old cowboy he knew as Tío Victor had slept during the final weeks of his life. Tío Victor had survived the early death of his one and only brother, the grandfather who had died almost ten years before the boy or any of his older siblings had been born.

At the top of the stairs, with his stomach turning summersaults, he sighs and takes solace because the bed he sleeps on is just a few steps away. In an effort to ignore the nausea that has begun rooting itself in his abdominal region, the boy tries to imagine what his melancholy Tío Victor might have been thinking during those final days when his health had begun to wane. Maybe the old man with a face that could have been carved from red stone had thought of the brother he'd lost while his nephew—eldest of his brother's three sons and the boy's father—had been far away in a country called Korea fighting in a war. The queasiness in his panza, forgotten for a moment, returns when he hears his mother shout from her door downstairs that it's time for them to come eat supper. Manolo is half way up when the boy turns around reluctantly and heads back down.

• • •

We moved to La Puente, a suburb of Los Angeles, in 1971. There, my father—never much of a church-goer—became a practicing Jehovah's Witness, embracing the religion his mom had adopted decades before. We attended Sunday services at a Kingdom Hall and were welcomed as a family. Soon enough, perhaps to bolster my father's nascent devotion, our home became the site of a weekly bible study led by a Mexican-American couple that had befriended my mom and dad at church. They sometimes brought one or two extended family members—a single sister-in-law or a nephew in high school—to encourage my older brother and oldest sister. They always brought along their son.

About a year or two older than I, he was tall for his age and had dark brown peach fuzz already sprouting on his upper lip. He reminded me of Eddie Haskell from Leave it to Beaver, a late '50s, early '60s television series in re-run syndication by then. Like the TV character, "Eddie" was always polite and well-behaved around grown-ups but a goofball cut-up when they weren't looking. Too young for the study group, we were allowed to play quietly in a bedroom at the end of the hallway.

When my younger sister came in holding a traditional doll—with a miniature plastic baby bottle and eyes that open and closed—clutched in one hand and a Barbie hanging from the other. "Eddie" talked her out of the Barbie easily by telling her that his mom was waiting in our kitchen with cookies made especially for her and her "baby." With the four-year-old safely out of the room, he turned to me with a grin and asked if I wanted to see Barbie's "tiggo bitties! Get it?! Big ol' titties?!" I had never paid much attention to women's breasts or their relative sizes, so I hadn't formed any opinions or preferences. I knew they were the source of breast milk, and had once heard a kid at school make fun a girl for wearing a "training bra." I was curious about Eddie's excitement and enthusiasm over the Barbie doll's unnatural *chichis*. He assured me that, beyond providing nutrition for babies, breasts were also part of "doing it," and that bigger was better. He swore that he had seen "lots of boobies" and had even touched one before. The revelation left me so stunned, it never occurred to me ask whose breast he had fondled.

As a second grader at California Elementary, I hadn't yet outgrown the notion that tugging on a girl's trenzas or her ponytail was the best way to let her know you liked her. As a self-proclaimed breast expert, Eddie had no trouble convincing me that Barbie's plastic breasts were ideal. I accepted the exaggerated tales of his exploits as gospel truth. It didn't matter if Barbie's "bazongas" had no nipples, he said, because those were just for nursing. Removing Barbie's one-piece swimsuit, he pointed to the prominent mounds below her narrow neck and dared me to kiss them, a suggestion that terrified and titillated me at the same time. I surprised him by accepting the dare and planting several smooches à la Pepé Le Pew on the doll's chest. He then dared me to put my pee-pee on them. "I'll do it if you do it," I said. "Okay, but you have to go first," he said. I agreed but insisted on going into the closet and leaving the door slightly ajar so he could keep watch and still confirm I'd made good on the dare with a quick look over his shoulder.

While I was zipping up my Toughskins pants—after I'd adjusted the end of my wee-wee to a position just inside my partially open fly so as to make as little actual contact with the Barbie breasts as possible—my older sister Anna charged loudly into the room. Full of suspicion, she demanded that Eddie tell her where I was and what we were doing. From inside, I saw him move in her direction, turn to face the closet and motion toward me with his head. The door flew open, and my shocked sister stood there frozen, her eyes wide and glaring. I stepped forward, nearly tumbling to the floor in an awkward effort to avoid a collision with her. Looking at the naked Barbie in my hand and my slightly unzipped trousers, she shouted, "Oooooh, boy!!! You're in big trouble now! I'm telling!!" Confronted by our respective parents, Eddie and I confessed to doing "mañas" with the Barbie doll, without mentioning the dare. Although Eddie had gotten away with welshing on the challenge, we both had to kneel in prayer and beg the Lord to forgive us.

I had never been so ashamed. After the Jehovah's Witnesses had gone, my father ordered my siblings out of the room, took out his belt, folded it in half and struck my rear end with it five or six times firmly. I tried to bear the whipping with quiet resolve, but my feelings of guilt and the reproach in his voice were too much. I broke down and cried uncontrollably. When he left the room, I hid my face in a corner, believing my behavior had marked me forever as a deviant, unworthy child. Word about how I'd put myself in time out must have reached my mother because it wasn't long before she came in with a slice of warm banana bread and a glass of milk. Wiping the tears from my eyes and face with a corner of her apron, she apologized for having slapped me several months earlier when I'd called my sister Anna a bitch. She wanted me to know that while my dad had administered stern discipline which was required, he had still expressed regret over the severity of his punishment. There were no further religious meetings in our home after that, and I'm sure it was because of the further humiliation my father suffered when Eddie's parents called to inform him that, according to their son, I had instigated the untoward conduct and led him into sin.

•••

"You alright, lil' primo?" Mano asks as the "School Boy" ducks by him toward the bottom of the stairs. Without looking back, the boy says, "I think I'm gonna throw up."

"Go to the restroom, foo! Splash some cold, cold water on your face and then turn the inside of your hands up like you're making a basket and let the water run over your wrists," the older boy hisses under his breath. "You gotta learn how to catch some snap." Luckily, the bathroom—with a door to his parents' room on one side and a door to the room where his sisters sleep on the other—is empty. In the dining room, his three older sisters are busy setting the table where they, his older brother and his parents always sit for supper. The boy, his six-year-old sister and his baby brother are relegated to a square table in the kitchen that looks out onto the spacious backyard. His mother stands in front of the stove with her back to the little kids' table warming the last of a dozen flour tortillas on a round cast iron comal.

"I don't feel so good, Mom. I think I need to go back to my room and lie down for a bit," he says. Laced together with his fingers, his hands are clasped in front right below his navel as if to subconsciously keep himself from doubling over. "Don't worry about making a plate for me," Turning away from the stove, she touches his forehead to check his temperature. "What's wrong, mi'jo? You don't have fever, but your face sure is red. Tienes que vomitar?" she asks. "A little bit. I got pretty queasy going up the stairs a minute ago, but it wasn't so bad coming down," he answers meekly. In the doorway to the kitchen behind him, Mano appears out of nowhere and interjects over the boy's shoulder. "It's my fault," he offers, "We ate a bunch of chips and candy. Plus we drank a large Cherry-flavored Slurpee mixed with a Coke-flavored one before we went swimming to Big Stacy Pool. Dispensa, Tía."

"He knows he shouldn't eat that stuff. Last year, he got sick and threw up for three days straight. He couldn't even keep water down. We had to take him to the emergency room." she says, her disapproval swelling in the silence that follows. "I'll give you some Bayer aspirin," she says finally with a softer, warmer tone. "Then you can go rest until you feel okay to come down and eat. You need to," she continues. "I don't want you to get up starving at one in the morning. Ya te conozco Monkey-Mouse… o kitchen mouse o quien sabe como te pusiste. Anyway, I know you'll act like a ninja, then wake everyone up down here poking around for food." The boy rolls his eyes while looking first at Mano then at her. "Amaaa-aá! Don't call me that!" he pleads with a heartbreaking desperation in his voice his mother does not recognize or remember. With a resolute sigh he continues, "That was a long time ago… in 2nd Grade. And it was Monkey-Man… that's what the letters I drew on the t-shirt stood for. It was stupid, I know… okay? But it wasn't Monkey-Mouse or kitchen mouse or any kind of mouse."

•••

A move to Austin after just two years in Southern California put us three hours from 'Buelita and Abuelito in Dewalt. Many of Grandma's large brood lived conveniently near her in small towns like Arcola, Sugarland and Missouri City. Some of their children, Micaela's grandkids and my first cousins, had already begun starting families themselves, branching out into Rosenberg, Richmond, East Bernard and Katy. Before moving to La Puente from the outskirts of Houston ourselves, we had been frequent guests at Grandma's house, dropping in on her and Abuelito at least twice a week. Back in Texas, however, our visits were curtailed. We spent the first year in a rental home on a corner that faced Fillmore Junior High athletic field, which began directly across the street and stretched out for an entire city block beyond that. My dad stayed behind in California for work and joined us in the new place a couple of months later.

The house behind ours faced a street that ran into the one which ran in front of ours and belonged to an elderly couple, Mr. and Mrs. Bushong. They took a liking to us and often hired my mom to help around the house. Mr. Bushong sometimes paid me to collect pecans produced by several trees in their large back yard. When the Bushongs decided it was time to find a place, which could provide assisted living services for them, a For Sale sign went up in their yard. My parents had gone to Houston, so my eldest sister tracked them down and called them with the news. When my father inquired, they offered to sell him their home themselves. It was clear they wanted us to have a place that was truly ours. Because the home was owner-financed, my father was not obligated to submit a credit score or deal with a mortgage bank at all.

My younger sister and I were so struck by the antique clear, cut-glass doorknobs in our new home that we pretended they were giant diamonds and played a game that involved listing all the things we would buy for one another and our parents after selling them. It was the nicest home we had ever really been inside, with a huge back yard and those pecan trees that rained down mountains of both hard-shell and soft-shell pecans for several months a year. Featuring glass-door cabinetry built into the two half walls that served as mantels separating the dining area from the living room, it included both a functional fireplace and a utility room with a washer and dryer. The house was like a dream come true. I could walk to my elementary school eight blocks away. And who wouldn't be happy collecting and shelling enough pecans for my mother to make her incredible homemade pecan pie?

The change that overcame my father once we'd closed on the property was nothing less than remarkable. He remained stern and his instructions, requests and commands would be the final word in our household forever. He was hot-headed, unapologetically macho and at times almost unforgivably sangrón, a word for someone who used cruel, cutting remarks as brutally as blows or as precisely as surgical incisions. But those traits were tempered by a sense of fairness, loyalty, duty and a gentlemanly charm. Once settled in the new house, much to our relief, his angry outbursts—which could end with hair-raising shouts or broken dinnerware flung into the sink—subsided drastically. He began to welcome visits from some of my mother's brothers and sisters and a number of her nieces and nephews who had already established their own families. Toting their rambunctious, wild-eyed country kids along by the carload, they all came eager to congratulate Tío Pete and Tía Julia.

Even 'Buelita—who rarely took time away from cooking for and picking up after the endless procession of relatives in and out of her front door—came to visit and offer us her blessing. My father seemed to like playing host at the spontaneous backyard barbecues many of these giddy reunions prompted. One gathering I remember specifically took shape because my cousin Elena had married a member of the well-known '70s era Mexican musical group Los Saylor's. My father was pleased to offer him the electric guitar he had given me for Christmas that we had stored in a closet for several months because we could not yet afford lessons. Because my two brothers were, respectively, seven years older and five years younger, I'd spent much of my childhood on adventures with imaginary friends. Although I played tag and Red Light Green Light with a sister two years ahead and card games like "Concentration" or Go Fish with a sister three years younger, I wanted to race bikes, build forts, play army and climb trees. So the occasional arrival of aunts, uncles and cousins with children closer to my age delighted me as much as it did my dad, if not more.

...

His eyes are closed, and he tries to banish the awful hallucinations hovering around him, lurking on the outer edges of his consciousness. He is afraid to fall asleep and has left the lights on in both rooms upstairs, cycling through a series of unrelated thoughts to keep his mind otherwise occupied. Though breathing and swallowing both aggravate his acute throat pain, he struggles to ignore it, fixating on the friends he has made at Bannister and looks forward to seeing again when the new school year starts. He's known Gabriel Moreno, Joel Castillo and Raymond Shaw since third grade. Oddly, he is compelled to offer a silent prayer asking God to ensure that Joel has been promoted. Of all the fourth-graders, Joel was the only person shorter than he was. "There's no way Joel got held back," he decides, convinced it is not his fate to become the shortest kid in Bannister Elementary 5th Grade Class. His peace is short-lived, unfortunately. His mind turns again to the unforgettable images and palpable fear from earlier that afternoon. His stomach growls loudly under his palms, adding yet another layer to his unrest.

After being excused from dinner, the boy had retreated meekly to his room and has seen or heard nothing of Mano since. Realizing that his cousin's absence has lent itself to a slight measure of relief in the midst of his turmoil, the door at the bottom of the stairs opens and closes with a noisy jolt. "Q'vo, little man! You still sleeping?" asks Mano once he reaches the top of the stairs. The boy sits up abruptly, slides his legs over the side of the bed and tries to pinpoint an unexpected yet welcome aroma. On one hand, the scent comforts him, raising his spirits instantly. On the other, it amplifies the magnitude and duration of the pangs now rumbling in his belly. Seeing him suddenly upright and sitting at the edge of the bed, Mano steps toward him, offering the younger boy a tall, bright red Tupperware tumbler with a lid and the napkin-wrapped fork. "Know how you're not supposed to eat up here? Well, trip out! While I'm snaking these from a pan inside the 'stufa, Tía Julia... your ma,' walks in catches me," Mano says. "She's pissed! But plays it off all cool and says just ask next time and she'll serve me seconds. I say 'Gracias Tía. That was serio, no lie, THE best enchilada dinner I ever ate anywheres. But these are for my little primo up there in his room, so he don't miss out. Or in case he wakes up with some mean munchies. That way he don't bug nobody coming down here.' Pretty smooth, right?"

Mano had been able to fit five enchiladas vertically in the tumbler in an attempt to smuggle them upstairs. The boy's mother had been touched enough by his gesture to fold a paper napkin around a fork herself before handing it to the post-adolescent houseguest. Suspending the regular house rule that prohibited food outside the dining room or kitchen for the enchilada care package, she had asked only that her new nephew not wake the boy if he was already sleeping. While her son had waited for her to administer the aspirin, he'd been unable to detect the rich spicy redolence emitted from the oven when his favorite meal was in the works. She knows the reverence with which he regards her culinary art, so she had known the minute he entered the kitchen that the severity of his tummy trouble was real.

The boy takes the tumbler and the fork from his step-cousin. Holding the tumbler in his left hand, he tears into the enchiladas as if to prevent them from being confiscated, leaving the fork in the cup occasionally to pick up the napkin on his lap and wipe the corners of his mouth. The napkin is useless before the third enchilada is finished. Unconsciously, he resorts to wiping with the back of his right hand—in which he holds the fork—until Mano grabs his wrist to stop him and drops the black bandana onto the boy's lap, picking up what's left of the paper napkin, balling it up and tossing it under the bed. The boy is so focused on the food he is oblivious to the fate of the soiled paper and proceeds, as before, using the cloth *paño* to mitigate the effect of his salivary glands in overdrive.

"I threw up *gacho* the first time I did glue and then the first time huffing paint," Mano confides. "I was a pee-wee, too." The boy winces at "peewee," but it doesn't bear the same sting as "school boy." The older boy has taken a seat next to him on the bed and throws an arm around the boy's neck in a mock wrestling headlock. Bending his fingers, he scrapes his knuckles against the top of the boy's head, giving him a light coscorrón, what some kids at school would call a "noogie." "But little man primo here didn't lose his shit at all!" his step-cousin says with pride. "I thought for sure you would throw up and get us busted."

Sensing the boy's discomfort, Mano lets go abruptly and stands. He motions toward a bookcase made from cinderblocks and wood planks. On it are his big brother's 8-track tapes, how-to books on drawing and model car building, old issues of Hot Rod magazine, a worn copy of Stuart Little, several Hardy Boys hard cover book, a Doc Savage paperback, a Doc Savage hardcover, and a box set of four paperbacks with all of the original Conan the Barbarian chronicles written by Robert E. Howard. His prize possession, the set was a Christmas gift from his second to oldest sister, Grace. "You read all these before? For reals?!" he asks. The boy has read everything on the shelf, several more Hardy Boys mysteries and even a Nancy Drew checked out of the Twin Maples library branch five blocks away. With his older brother, he has started reading Huckleberry Finn. "My brother reads two pages and I read one. When he reads the parts where Huckleberry Finn is talking, he does it different, like he's Huck. When he says words like 'pappy' and 'injun,' it's funny," the boy exclaims.

The boy pulls a flashlight and a hardcover volume from under the corner of the mattress to prove he is not making it up. Under the sheet, which the older boy has pulled over them both, he switches on the flashlight and opens the book to a page marked by a folded corner. He reads aloud in a voice barely above a whisper, and after only three pages, he hears his step-cousin snoring beside him. Turning off the flashlight, he turns onto his right side, shuts the book and slides the flashlight between the wall and the bed. With the closed book under his left hand, he slides his right arm under the pillow and drifts into sleep dreaming of a raft on a river. The precarious wooden vessel is tossed and rocked by waves and hidden currents.

Roused by movement and rustling sounds, he is no longer on the raft. Groggy, he comes to, feeling the pressure of weight on top of his small frame. He is face down on the bed, his forehead resting on the edge of the pillow, his arms reaching underneath it instinctively, pulling it deliberately towards him. Soundlessly, he buries his face within its folds. His shorts have been pulled down to just below his knees. The teenager is breathing heavily behind him but makes no other noise as moves his hips back and forth. There is something foreign and strange pushing against him down there. It is Mano in the final throes of a release. At once alert and fearful, he pretends to sleep then disassociates, abandoning his body, leaving it inert, the school boy becoming Raggedy

Andrés, Raggedy Anne's Mexican-American brother. His step-cousin rolls away with a muted sound like a whimper. Slowly, the boy makes his way back to the empty shell, the limp body he has vacated. Wearing his skin once again, he feels something else, a thick liquid he does not yet know about or understand as ejaculate inside his bottom.

He remains motionless, feigning sleep for the ensuing hours, until a gray light appears in the window on the wall next to where his head rests on the pillow. He pulls his swim shorts up and inches his way downward to the foot of the bed like a worm. Digging a pair of pants out of a dresser in the otherwise empty room where Tío Victor lived briefly, he pulls them up over his swim trunks and heads downstairs as quietly as he can. His parents are awake but still in bed.

"Mi'jo, are you feeling better?" his mother asks. "Yes, 'Amá," he answers. "But I have to use number two and then take a bath. Can I watch cartoons after if I turn the sound all the way down?" His father, surprised to hear the boy uncharacteristically assert himself and his intent to bathe at such an early hour, is so impressed that he interjects with definitive permission. "Go ahead and watch your cartoons or whatever you like, son. It's okay to use the volume, too, as long as you keep it really low, okay?"

"Thank you, Dad. I will," he answers.

For the first time ever, he fills the tub with the warmest water he can stand, turns off the faucet and—wearing his trunks—lowers himself into it. After getting used to the heat, he turns the hot water on and slides forward on his back until his face is submerged. Holding his breath and listening for his heartbeat, he counts to 45 silently, comes up for air knowing he could easily have waited 15 second more and turns the hot water off. Dressed, he wrings out the wet trunks and hangs them on a towel rack, pours himself a bowl of cereal in the kitchen and sits on the carpeted living room floor to watch Looney Tunes. When his family begins moving about, he puts his half-eaten bowl of cereal in the sink and leaves to wander around the junior high campus across the street swing listlessly from chin-up bars outside the tennis courts in the school yard before heading back home. Before reaching his house, he shimmies up a tall narrow tree with branches that can only be reached after a strenuous climb. It is rooted in the earth between the sidewalk and the curb. Reaching a branch sturdy enough to hold him but high enough to keep him hidden in its foliage, he lets his legs and arms dangle freely on either side of it. Later, he sees his step-cousin look for him, stopping other kids on the street to ask where he is. Heading toward the school, Manolo walks directly beneath him but does not look up.

From his perch high above ground, the boy can see past privacy fences into back yards, into second story windows and even across the occasional rooftop. The tree has offered solace and refuge before; its shaded, cool surfaces and bright foliage provide him cover and camouflage while its height and strength give him ample footholds, nooks and hand-rests leading all the way to the top. If he climbs higher, he will be more visible to others but will be able to see more of the surrounding streets and homes, something he has always wanted to do. Today, however, he is content to disappear into the tree like a troll. He crosses his arms to form a cradle for his cheek against the branch supporting his upper torso. Feeling several drops of what he thinks is an oncoming case of the sniffles pooling at the edge of his nose, he ignores them. If he waits, with his compact 40-pound body draped cat-like over the stout tree limb, the watery *mocos*, or sinus drainage will just fall to the street, he figures.

"Besides, I'm a mild-mannered elementary student by day and Monkey-Man, superhero crime-fighter by night," he says softly and half-heartedly to himself. Nobody will even see them. And if they do, they won't know it came from his leaky nose because they can't even see him, he reasons. The blistering Hill Country sun is midway in the sky when he hears the faint sound of his name. Someone at home is calling him. They must be looking for him because lunch is ready. Instinctively, he wipes his nose with the back of his left hand and automatically dries it on the leg of his trousers. To carry out the maneuver, he's grabbed the bottom of the branch where his chest is balanced with his right hand, bending the elbow and using that arm as a counterweight to keep himself steady. He notices the traces of blood on the back of his left index and middle fingers with a start. Shifting his gaze upward, he wonders if he is sharing the tree with an injured animal or bird.

Out of nowhere and so suddenly that he reacts with a startled jerk, he hears a familiar voice coming from below. "Hello?! Excuse me?! Mr. Monkey-Man?! Hey, you! I'm down here!!" says his younger sister Perla Elizabeth in an articulate, matter-of-fact tone that grows louder the longer her greeting goes unanswered from above. The boy looks down and waves to let her know he sees her and is listening. "How's the air up there? Are you after some dastardly villain or criminal mastermind? Should we be alarmed?" she asks with more sincerity than sarcasm. Perla is a second-grader in the gifted class at Bannister. The two of them walk to and from school together, and she has proven herself adept at expanding on some of his more fanciful, made-up adventure stories. Today, he is strangely grateful for his bright little sister's reference to an imaginary role he'd been ready to let go forever the night before during the discussion in the kitchen with his mom, the character he'd invoked wistfully a mere seconds before. It is as if she is reading his mind. "Everything seems to be okay, Ms. Elizabeth. But we'll keep you posted," he responds. "We're doing our best to keep the streets safe for good eggs like you and your family, ma'am."

"Well, on that subject, if you happen to see my brother, could you please tell him everyone is looking for him and that my mom needs to see him right away. They're worried because he's been gone since very early this morning and no one can find him," she continues. "Anna or Grace found a can of spray paint in the garage and someone, not me, tattled. So if you see him, let him know he needs to get home." Several neighborhood kids and curiosity seekers have begun to gather around Perla, drawn by the peculiar manner in which she speaks, looking back and forth at the siblings as if they were aliens from another planet. Stepping up onto the curb in the direction of their home a couple of houses down, she ignores them, and still looking up at him, says, "By the way, your nose is bleeding."

Before the boy can even bring his hand to his nose to confirm what he has just been told, he sees a thin strand of blood fall—almost as if in slow motion—to the street below. The small crowd of those assembled closes in but retreats when the blood strikes the asphalt surface. None want to be within range of the spontaneous nosebleed erupting overhead. He can hear exclamations and murmurs and shrieks from the onlookers standing underneath him. They will echo in his head for years to come.

...

EPILOGUE

I wish the things described here had never happened or weren't true. I wish some of the things that happened after the things described in this story hadn't happened or weren't true. But they did and they were. The specific conversations may not have unfolded the way they have been written, but all of the events and situations were real and unforgettable. After descending from my treetop sanctuary, I faced my mother and confessed that my step-cousin and I had been trying to sniff paint and had instead huffed gasoline. She responded by slapping me with unexpected fury. My step-cousin was placed on a bus and sent home. It turned out that while I'd been hiding in the tree, he'd gone around threatening all of the kids in the neighborhood with bodily harm if they so much as looked at me wrong. I did not have the courage to tell anyone what had transpired in my room the night before until many years later.

Sharing the recollection of abuse at the hands of a step-cousin I never saw again when I heard he had been killed in a drive-by shooting with a sibling, I did realize I would inadvertently invite suspicion upon myself. I had become a favored uncle among my nieces and nephews and was particularly close to my younger half-brothers. My father's sons from a second marriage, they were three and six respectively, when the younger of the two innocently told me that he had been instructed not to be near me or play with me when there were no other adults in the room. I was 19-years-old and a student at the University of Texas by then. Romantically, I was involved with a much older woman who was a city arts commissioner and had come to see me in a community theater production she had voted on funding for. I had, after the incident which had taken place during my own childhood, found my way out of the trauma by way of the arts as an actor on a bilingual PBS television series I was cast in when I was 12-years-old and a 7th Grader at the neighboring junior high. In high school, I had embraced academics, athletics and theater.

Hearing my youngest sibling—whom I would have taken, and would still, take a bullet for—say that he and his older brother had been warned to stay away from me was a blow to my psyche nearly equal to the molestation that I had suffered at nine. After some discreet inquiries, I learned that two of my sisters and my mother were deeply concerned about the possibility that I had or perhaps would continue the cycle. I was devastated, and, at one point, broke down in tears to my father, who called my mother and told her how profoundly I had been hurt by the suspicion and indirect accusation that I was capable of repeating what had been done to me.

One of my sisters met me in the rental house where I was living to ask if I had experienced any urges and recommended counseling, informing me that none of the children in our family she interviewed had reported any inappropriate sexual contact. She confessed that she herself had once initiated such with me when I was a boy, using her foot, a contact that had obviously been so brief I had absolutely no memory of it. My mother met me in a park overlooking the river, which ran through the middle of town. We shared lunch on a park bench. She apologized for not having protected me enough to prevent what had happened to me as a child and that she loved me more than life itself. We cried together, and I told her that neither she nor my father were to blame, that I loved her just as much in return. All of my creative energy as well as a love for the arts and my gifts or inclinations as a fledgling poet and a writer, I said, had come down to me from her. I also told her that I was ready to forgive my abuser, even though he was no longer living. She suggested in response that I forgive myself because I was also blameless and had not invited the abuse.

As of this writing, over a rainy L.A. weekend late January, 2019, I've realized that the nosebleed in the tree was both a reaction to the trauma of abuse and the result of mucus membrane tissue damage inside my nostrils from the gasoline fumes I'd inhaled. In the process of recovering these memories, I have also not only forgiven myself, but have also let go of so many ghosts and fears that have lingered. I have likewise determined that I will forgive my step-cousin posthumously. Because of him, I grew closer to my sisters and learned to appreciate all they represented in my own development as an artist and a human being. I spoke to the two oldest to let them know I would be sharing this chronicle, and they both wished me well, expressing their love for me and their pride at my willingness to address a difficult, very personal subject. Male friends have congratulated me on my bravery and fortitude, sharing similar experiences they had never spoken of before and which I would never have imagined. It is my sincerest and most tender wish that this conversation continue and that, as men, we begin to understand ourselves and our truest place in the universe as brothers, fathers, sons, partners and friends. Only through this will we finally empower ourselves to be the change we want to see.

"I will have my voice: Indian, Spanish, white. I will have my serpent's tongue - my woman's voice, my sexual voice, my poet's voice. I will overcome the tradition of silence."

Gloria E. Anzaldúa

Brenda Xavez
Poet, Visionary, Mother & Community Activist

Brenda Xavez is a poet, writer and first generation Chicana. From an early age, books and school were her refuge. In high school, she was awarded a scholarship to attend Windward, a prestigious college preparatory school. She then graduated from Stanford and Columbia Law School. Ms. Xavez is an incest and rape survivor. Despite these violations, she is grateful for her life and hopes to be a source of light and healing, especially for survivors. She is grateful for her mom, Juanita, her son, Extli, her pareja, David, her second father, Dick, and all who helped her healing journey, especially Juanita, Maria Elena, Vrisa, Ernestine, Yasmin and her women's group.

MI TESTIMONIO: A STORY OF SURVIVAL AND HEALING

I was born into a long line of women and men who have been violated: sexually, physically and otherwise. I am the product of conquest: the conquest perpetrated by Spaniards over indigenous brown bodies and the conquest of my father over my mother—when he kidnapped and raped her— before my brother and sister were born, before I was born.

Hot breath of whiskey and menthol cigarettes on neck and breasts as he pins wrists against bed. Sweaty stomach against uterus. Weight against heart. She closes her eyes. Holds her breath as he thrusts against her. This, the first violation by future husband.

My story, my mother's story and even my father's story, is descended from and connected, through the generations and the suffering and the beatings, to Coyolxauhqui's story and how she became the Aztec moon goddess. Before us, before our suffering, there was Coatlicue, Aztec earth goddess and mother to all gods. As this creation myth goes, Coatlicue is expecting a child that Coyolxauhqui learns will bring suffering and death. His name is Huitzilopochtli and he is the god of war. Coyolxauhqui conspires with her four hundred brothers and sisters, who are the stars, to kill Coatlicue and prevent Huitzilopochtli's birth. Huitzilopochtli is warned of his sister's plan when he is in his mother's womb. When Coyolxauhqui approaches her mother to kill her, Huitzilopochtli is miraculously born in full warrior gear and battles his sister. He manages to cut off her limbs and beheads her, banishing her head to the sky where

Coyolxauhqui becomes the moon goddess. This battle between brother and sister, between male and female, between patriarchy and matriarchy, re-enacts itself every day with the birth of the sun and the moon.[1]

Betrayed by mother, her heart breaks into hundreds of pieces, as spirit leaves body, blood spilling from severed head flung to the night sky.

My maternal grandfather was a cruel man. I grew up hearing stories of how he savagely beat my grandmother- and the kids- the ten who survived infancy. My grandmother, a battered wife, in turn would beat her children and curse at them, injuring their bodies and spirits. One day my grandfather abandoned the family- a relief for them, from his beatings. However, my grandmother was left alone to feed all those hungry mouths. She was an illiterate indigenous woman already living in poverty and turned a blind eye to signs that her daughters were being raped by her eldest daughter's husband. A man who provided her with financial support.

"¡Nos vendiste!" my Tia Flor recalls yelling at her eldest sister during an argument, years after their mother's death. "You sold us!" I gasped for breath when I heard my Tia tell this story. My heart beat quicker as I pictured this confrontation between sisters- a breaking of the silence.

Anger boils in her veins, delivered to every part of her: skin, feet, fists, mouth, even tips of hair, stomach, heart and always to her left side. The anger makes her want to kick and punch and scream but she does nothing, silenced by betrayal, she does nothing.

---

1 I first heard this story in Cherríe Moraga's class when I was in college and would like to thank her for introducing me to this origin myth and her feminist interpretation of it, which has impacted my life in so many ways. There are numerous variations of this story that survived the Spanish conquest of the indigenous people of the Americas. The source for the main points in this version can be found at https://www.ancient.eu/Coyolxauhqui/.

The youngest daughter in the family, my Tia Magdalena, remembers standing guard outside the concrete structure where she shared one bed with all her sisters. She crouched on the tin roof of the opposite structure, hiding from view as best she could, armed with rocks- big rocks, sharp rocks- in her twelve-year-old hands. She threw them at him- this first rapist- as he approached the structure. The rapist later told on her and my grandmother beat my Tia Magdalena: punched, pulled, kicked, cursed, dragged, blood splattering on dark earth, as my grandmother hung her from a tree.

Heart pounds in hot and swollen ears. Face fills with blood. Eyes feel like they will pop out from the pressure. She shuts them, her eyes, as scalp throbs where hair was pulled from its roots. Pain, burning pain, searing pain, of heart breaking into hundreds of pieces as spirit leaves body.

I listened to these stories as my *tias* and *tios*- aunts and uncles- swapped horror stories across the kitchen table, uncensored stories, oblivious to my listening ears. I think I first felt my mother's sadness when I was still in her womb and ingested it when she breastfed me. By the time I was born, thirteen years into my parent's marriage, my father no longer beat my mother; for the most part, she was a compliant and submissive battered wife.

Sister battles brother, swinging her macuahuitl in defense of self and countless innocent men, women and children who will perish with the coming of war. She uses her chimalli to block swings aimed to kill her and the uprising against his patriarchy. Mother stands by his side, complicit in her silence. Coyolxauqui looks at her, eyes pleading with her to understand, to help stop the bloodshed. Instead of helping, mother looks away, signaling son to finish battle. Betrayed by mother,

Coyolxauhqui's heart breaks into hundreds of pieces and in that moment of betrayal, during the blue period between day and night, his macuahuitl strikes her left leg first, severing limb from joint. She is numb from shock as he continues using wooden club with sharp obisidian blades to sever left arm next, then right leg and right arm. Her fingers still attached to left hand on severed arm finally open and drop her shield, its feathers soaking with her red blood. Fingers on severed right hand also loosen and drop her wooden club, black obsidian blades glistening with her dark blood. He looks down at sister, her eyes shedding tears, heart broken, as red blood splatters across sky and soaks into brown earth from open wounds. Mother watches as he delivers final blow to neck, severing head from body. He picks up sister's head, grabbing black hair in right hand and swings it to the sky. Mother sheds tears but watches and does nothing.

I am four years old and sitting on the couch next to my father. It is nighttime and we are watching a Spanish language variety show on television. This woman, a very voluptuous woman, dressed in a sequined bathing suit comes on the screen. She has curly long dark hair. She smiles for the camera as she dances and her large breasts jiggle under her tight black suit. The television hosts introduces her as Iris Chacon. In the darkness of the living room, my father leans in and tells me, *"No quieres hacer hezo para mi?"* / "Don't you want to do that for me?" I look at him in the darkness, his face and glasses illuminvated by the gray blue light from the television. I don't understand what he means. My heart beats loudly in my chest and ears.

At this moment, bathed in fear, her heart breaks into hundreds of pieces, as spirit leaves body.

I don't say anything to my father. I can't. I am frozen as I hold my breath and shift my weight, making myself smaller under his penetrating gaze.

I am five years old and my playmates are Rosa and Ana who are one year older and one year younger than me. My mom tells me she babysits them so that I will have playmates, my older siblings, teenagers by then, being generally absent from my life and the house. We are dancing for my father. He sits on a vinyl kitchen chair, clapping for us as we play dress up for him. We change clothes, swap dresses inside the bathroom and open the door to dance and strip for him, a smile on his lips. His eyes light up behind his slightly tinted glasses. Ana, the youngest, does not want to participate. She crouches in the corner of the bathroom, crying "no", sobbing as she buries her head in between her small knees. Rosa and I taunt her for not wanting to participate and call her a cry baby. I am jealous of Rosa, of the way that my father looks at her and how his eyes light up when she dances for him. When it is my turn, I raise my skirt higher than she does- I am not wearing underwear- and part my lips for him. He claps in delight and lets out a chuckle, savoring the moment.

Tiny hands disappear into nothingness. There is a void where heart used to be, where spirit used to be. She grinds her teeth in the darkness. Holds breath as limbs and torso become numb, break apart, disappear under his weight, hot breath, leathery skin and thick fingers.

I am a woman now and sick and vomiting with food poisoning in the apartment I share with my son and mother. I spend most of the night in the bathroom, the nausea hitting my body in violent waves. Finally, after hours of agonizing pain, I am exhausted but feel well enough to go lay down. My son is sleeping and I do not want to disturb him in the room we share. I make my way to the living room and lay down on the couch. It is almost the blue period. I can see the darkness outside the living room window starting to change, the faint rays of light blending into night, gradually making the darkness lighter. I am laying on my side in a fetal position and start to doze off. In this half-wake, half-sleep state, I see an old brown woman, with long white hair and a white flowing nightgown. I feel warmth in my heart. She spoons me on the couch, holding me in her arms. I feel safe and loved. When I open my eyes, I realize that my heart knows her. I recognize that she has always been with me. I now know that I was never alone. I think of this whenever I remember the loneliness, the anger and the abandonment.

Spirit woman holds her small hand, shields brown eyes with long white hair, as toddler body is being prodded, held against will by thick fingers, big hands, sweaty big belly against heart. She sees nothing, feels nothing, as spirit woman takes her away.

My father has promised to buy me a doll in exchange for my silence. I am watching cartoons in the living room and a commercial comes on advertising this big ballerina doll. The doll stands on one leg, the other leg is bent at the knee and forms a triangle as she rests her foot against the standing leg. The doll stretches her arms above her head, the palms face each other as the elbows slightly bend. She is on a special stand that spins her around when you press a button. She is wearing a pink leotard and tutu. My father is in the living room with me when the commercial comes on. I point to the doll and tell him that that's the doll I want. He nods and agrees to buy it for me. Months later, I remind him of his promise and eventually he buys me a doll at the swap meet. She is not the ballerina doll. This doll is a blonde doll made with cheap plastic and stiff arms and legs. I still play with her and remain silent.

She retreats into herself, playing with dolls and later, when she is older, into the world that books provide her. She feels alone, so alone, wishing for a connection to self, to body. Anger is her constant companion, searing under skin, exposing filth and hatred inside her.

I am part of a women's group. We are reading a book to help us find romantic love. It is a seven week course that involves writing exercises and various assignments, meant to heal our hearts. I am in my thirties, a single mother and want to find a life partner. I want a healthy relationship. This week's assignment includes writing a letter to my child self. As I contemplate what I will write her, three and four-year-old me, I get a vision of pictures of me at that age in the family albums. I now recognize that those pictures were part of my father's grooming process. I want to gather them. I do not want to destroy them. I want to give them love. I want to give her love. I envision putting a nice ribbon around them. I envision putting them in a nice box. I do not question the vision but decide to honor it and follow my heart. I gather my strength and go through the family albums, warm tears streaming down my face. I find a series of pictures of me at three or four years old. It is a photo shoot taken in our living room, in the house I grew up in. It is day time. I wear different outfits in the pictures. In some I wear wigs. In one I am in my underwear and am laying face down on a big flowered patterned cushion. My mouth is open, as the side of my face presses against the cushion. My eyes look down. I see my still chubby hand in the picture and my still chubby legs, the hand and legs of a toddler becoming a child. Part of my body is in shadows and part of my body is illuminated by harsh light streaming through the big window facing the front of the house. In another picture I am sitting down in an arm chair. I hold a huge squash on my lap from our vegetable garden. The squash hides the upper part of my body and the bottom part of my face. My legs are crossed. The left leg raised so that you can see the back of my thigh and that I am wearing pink shorts underneath the summer dress. My soft brown eyes stare back at me. I want to let her know that I know. That she was never alone.

No estas sola mi chiquita. Estoy aqui contigo. Nunce estuviste sola. You were never alone.

I gather all the pictures I find. There is a picture of Rosa and I sitting next to each other in Halloween outfits. I am wearing a long black dress, make-up and a long black wig. I remember I was supposed to be Elvira, Mistress of the Dark. I sit crossed legged in the picture, my legs exposed, a white garter belt on my right thigh. We are smiling in this picture. The stamped date on the picture says it was taken in 1984, when I was seven years old. There is also a picture of my mom opening birthday presents in the living room. She is sitting on the floor, a big smile on her lips, as she holds a pink and white dress up for her guests to view. I sit across from her, along with some of her friends and a neighbor and friend of my father's. This family friend later went to jail for sexually assaulting his daughter. I don't have any memories of him assaulting me but I know that he and my father would spend time together- fellow pedophiles and rapists- and that this family friend would visit often. There is one picture of me on my parent's bed. One of the red curtains covering the front windows is drawn shut. The one next to it is only partially closed. Daylight seeps in and illuminates a dresser next to a window. I am about five years old. I am in my underwear and wear white socks and blue dirty tennis shoes. I sit on my knees and lean into the pillows at the top of the bed, holding my upper body up with my outstretched hands. There is another camera on the bed, underneath my bare chest. My mouth is partially open. My soft brown eyes look scared and confused. You can see my crib in the background, against the windows facing the front of the house.

We are playing dress up for him and are in the bedroom I share with my older sister. We haven't started the game yet and are picking out outfits. I call the blue gown I recently wore as a flower girl. It is a puffy long blue dress and one of my favorites to wear for him.

I've waited for a day when I am alone in my apartment. My son, who recently turned five years old, is spending the night with his dad as part of our co-parenting arrangement. I gather the pictures. I cry for her, for little me. I tell her I love her. I light the candle on my altar. It is a white candle that rests between a statute of Coatlicue and a statute of La Virgen, the Mexican brown virgin Mary. I use sage to cleanse the pictures and the other items I've gathered for the occasion. Among these items is a box I repurpose. It is a white gift box and a blank canvas for me. The words "baby made with love" are printed on one side of the lid. I follow my heart and instincts for the next few hours. During this time, I sit at my son's kid table in the middle of the living room and write little me a letter. I seal the envelope and write: "with love... to my beautiful girl child... Brendita" on it. I take out drawing paper and draw a picture using my son's colored pencils. The drawing is of a little girl child living out in the forest. I draw a mushroom house next to her, with heart flowers coming out of the roof and popping out of the grass. She is a wild child, with long brown hair and a big smile on her lips. She stands next to a big tree, its branches reaching to the sky and roots reaching down to the earth. I use stickers to decorate the drawing and box. I use glittery stars, butterflies and flower stickers. I place a sticker on the top of the lid that says "made with love." I draw rainbows and a big butterfly. I do all of this with love, lots of love for her- and for me. As I sit in one of my son's little chairs, drawing on the table, I realize that she is in the room with me now, sitting across from me in the other little chair. I don't see her but I feel her presence. I start talking to her. Telling her I am glad she has joined me.

She is little- about four or five years old. Her hair is short, like it was at that time. She sits quietly across from me, her little hands on the table.

We gather all the materials I bought for the occasion, which includes a doll. It's a small doll, wearing a little gray sweater and a pink ruffled shirt. She wears pink stockings and pink shoes. We decide to use a sharpie and mark the letter "B" for "Brendita" under one of her shoes. Brendita has long brown hair and a hair tie with a pink flower in it. I hold her close to my heart. We gather the drawing, the letter, Brendita and a small stuffed animal of Scooby-Doo that I bought, because I used to love watching Scooby-Doo as a little girl. I want to add something else and find a blue glittery butterfly to add to the box. I go to my altar and pick out a small hawk feather. I add the feather to the bundle of pictures and wrap the bundle in yellow ribbon. We sage again and pray for mother earth to heal us. I use holy water that a good of friend of mine brought me from an overseas trip. I spray the box with a mist spray called "Open Heart" made by a healer in my community. We place the box on top of my son's kid table. I take out my journal and start writing about the experience. As I finish writing, I realize that she is still here with me. I decide to honor her presence and treat her like I do my son, like I wish I was treated as a child. I tell her she is beautiful and deserving of love, healthy love. I put out my hand for her to hold and bring her to the couch with me. I lay her across my lap and breastfeed her. *Le hablo de cariño.* I talk to her in baby talk. I call her *"mi chiquita"*— my little one — and sing to her as she breastfeeds. I picture her in my arms, and put out my arm to hold her head up. I picture her small hand reaching up to me as I nourish her. She looks at me with her soft brown eyes, vulnerable, loving, safe. I sing to her and love her. I lose track of time as I hold her and feed her and heal her.

My milk runs through her body, ingested through mouth, into stomach and heart. It travels through her little body, to skin, feet, hands, torso, and to her left side, the deeply wounded side, and fills the holes—the voids—with love.

I become conscious of the time and decide to start getting ready for my evening outing with friends. I tell Brendita I must go out for the night but that she will be safe here. I carry her in my arms, feeling her chest and beating heart against mine. I walk down the hallway to the bedroom and tuck her into our bed. I sing to her and give her a stuffed bear to sleep with. I lean in to kiss her and assure her she is safe and loved here. I leave the night light on for her before heading out.

Her wounds are healing. The severed skin and flesh, where the obsidian blades cut through joints, muscles and arteries, have now stopped bleeding.

The next morning, I drive out to Azusa to pick up my son from his dad's house. A good friend of mine has invited us to her baby shower. It is a big party, held at a salon. As I take my son out of his car seat, I realize that Brendita is with us. In my mind's eye, I take off her seat belt as well. As I walk into the salon, holding my son's hand, I physically hold out my hand for Brendita to hold. She is wearing a pretty dress, her hair is short like it was in the pictures. She is happy. I feel her little fingers in my hand. Later at the party, when I bring out my son to the dance floor, I see Brendita coming with us as I hold her little hand in my other hand. As I dance and spin my son on the dance floor, I hold out my other hand for Brendita, imagining that she is spinning with us. We laugh and smile as we heal together. It's been three years since the first time Brendita first appeared to me. Although her presence has never been as palpable as it was that first weekend, I know she is here with me now. I am happy to care for her and tell her I love her and send her love, especially on days when I am triggered.

Her skin is cut, flesh bleeding from the wounds on her arms. I tell her I love her. I tell her she is safe now. Blood stops spilling as her heart begins to mend, one broken piece at a time.

I am on the metro with my son, heading to Santa Monica. We are on the Gold Line and need to transfer trains at Union Station in order to make our way to the beach. My son still uses a stroller but there are a couple of seats available in the train car and my son sits in one of the empty chairs. I put the brakes on the stroller and place it next to our seats. I sit next to my son and watch him play with his action figures. It is a clear day in Los Angeles as the train makes its way into Downtown. I look over at my son who is sitting to my left and all of a sudden, I see an image of myself at his age in bed with my father. It is nighttime, the lights are out. The image is a close up of bodies. My body is naked. He is behind me, sweaty, big belly against my back. I feel his breath on my left ear. I don't know what is happening. I am confused. I am scared. I feel alone, severely alone. An empty void creeps into my heart. I become numb.

Tightness in throat. I cannot breathe. Fat bare stomach, sweaty stomach, on back. Hot breathe on ear, sucking, wetness. I cannot breathe. On their bed. Nighttime. No lights. Tightness in throat. I cannot breathe. Thick fingers on right shoulder. Hot breathe on ear. Slimy tongue. Wet lips on ear. I cannot breathe.

The next stop is Union Station, our stop. I cannot get the images out of my mind. My body wants to scream, yell, kick. My skin burns. For many years, while I was in therapy, I wanted to know everything that happened. I remembered the dancing and my body remembered that there was more- but I did not have any images, I did not have those memories. After years of on and off therapy, including individual and group therapy, I finally gave up wanting to know. In fact, I actually became thankful that the universe spared me the visual details, although my body always remembered. Here I am, now a mother, and years since I last saw a therapist and out of the blue and without my consent- the images popped into my head and my body knew that this was my truth. My stomach knots and I feel nauseous. I look over at my son and wonder whether we should head back home but he is so happy and excited about our excursion to Santa Monica. We have been there before and he is looking forward to playing in the kid's play area at the Promenade.

Behind me, thick fingers, forcing legs open, sitting between his legs. Wet tongue on left ear. No clothes. No clothes. Father, behind. Mamá no estas. Mamá no esta.

I cannot go back. I gather my son and sit him in the stroller. As I exit the train and head for the elevator on the platform, there are hundreds of voices screaming in my head. My voices- my girl child voices. I feel pain in my throat. Every inch of my body burns. I push the stroller with fists because I want to punch. I cannot straighten my fingers to grasp the handle. I don't know how I'm able to breathe. I don't know how I'm able to walk. But I do. I push the stroller and attempt to loosen my fist but the fingers will not listen. I push the stroller with my fists, down the tunnel, heading towards the Red Line. I start using exercises I've learned in therapy, asking myself to tune into present. What do I hear? What do I see? What do I smell? Asking my body, begging it to be in my present. As we enter the main lobby of Union Station, I finally begin to hear the noises around me, people walking by on cell phones or talking with their companions. I smell the sweet smell of baking bread and grilling meat as we pass a pretzel and hotdog stand.

I almost miss it but I soon begin to hear the faint sounds of a piano getting louder. There is a piano in the lobby at Union Station, part of a temporary art project, left there for passengers to use. People are gathered at the piano listening to a man playing passionate music. I make my way to the crowd and stop the stroller at the edge of the circle. I listen, really listen to the notes. I follow them with my heart. Slowly, my heart stops racing, my fists start to loosen. I feel the firm tile floor underneath me. I feel that I have been perspiring and that the underarms of my shirt are wet. I feel the wet cotton against my skin. I feel that I am wearing shorts and that they are a little loose on my thighs. I feel that I am wearing sandals and feel a breeze on the tops of my feet. I feel that my hair is pulled up in a ponytail. I continue listening to the music, letting it wash over me and through me as it melts away the screams and burning. I feel myself breathing, existing in this moment. I am alive and here, in Union Station, listening to this wonderful piano player and my son is here, watching him too. I still see the images of my father and little me for the rest of the day, close ups of skin, arm, feel hot breath on ear but these images and sensations do not break me.

Her body freezes under his weight. Her limbs go numb, legs unable to move, arms unable to stop his hands, fingers. Her throat numbs from pain, gasping for breath in between thrusts, as tears stream down face, heart breaking into hundreds of pieces. Numbness, darkness, as spirit leaves body.

At the end of the day and back home, I feel raw and exhausted. I know that this too will pass. I am grateful to be alive, to be here with my son, to love him and let him know that he is loved, to have him safe in my arms as he closes his eyes and falls asleep. I tell Brendita she is safe too. I tell her I am with her.

She joins us on the bed. As I hold my son in my arms, she sits next to us. I put out my arm for her. She settles her little body next to my son's, resting her head next to his, on my chest. She feels safe here, with us. She is deeply wounded but our love heals her, slowly mending her broken heart, allowing the blood to clot and finally stop bleeding. Body forms new tissue over cuts, scrapes and punctures on skin. Her hands no longer form fists, the fingers allow mine to hold them as I bring her hand to my heart and she feels the beating of life and oxygen to self.

I push my son's stroller towards the gathering at This Is Not a Cornfield, at the northern part of Los Angeles State Historic Park. My mom is with me and walks next to us. My son fell asleep on the way here, lulled by the swaying of the metro train as it made its way towards Chinatown. I have been invited to a day time indigenous ceremony. An Afro-Caribbean dance troupe is hosting the ceremony. There are healers from different circles here, including Aztec ceremonial *danzantes* and elders from different tribes. We arrive after the ceremony has already started. There are people gathered in a big circle on the dirt floor. The Afro-Caribbean dance troupe is playing drums and dancing, the lively music engulfing all the participants. The dancers are dressed in all white, loose fitting clothing. There is a woman leading the ceremony. She speaks to the crowd, asking everyone to join and dance with them. As people from the crowd enter the circle, I decide to participate. My mom stays with my son, who is still asleep in his stroller, along with others who are forming the perimeter of the circle. I allow myself to move to the rhythms of the drums, the rattles and various African and indigenous instruments. The woman dances while she speaks to the crowd, her load voice carrying across the field and above the sounds of drums and rattles. All around me people are swaying, moving to the sounds of the music. There are children and elders here. People are smiling and laughing, moving their arms, hips and feet to the rhythm of the drums or the rhythm of their hearts. The woman is speaking about the power of the sun to heal and calling upon our ancestors to join us. She asks us to raise our arms to the sky and to feel the energy of the sun and the moon and the stars. She expresses her gratitude to the ancestors who are here with us. I raise my arms, along with all the others. I listen to her speak of gratitude and healing. She asks us to look up and open our hearts. I feel the heat of the sun on my face and my arms. I feel the pulsing rhythm of the drums coming up from mother earth, up my body, through my feet. I look up at the sky and open my heart. I picture my heart connected to the sun.

She looks up at the sky, feels the hot sun on her skin, and prays for mother earth to heal her.

The woman tells us to ask the universe for what is in our hearts. She tells us to ask and raise our arms higher. At that moment, as I look up at the blue gray sky and raise my arms higher, I hear myself say "*Te perdono*/I forgive you". Immediately I know it is about him, my father. My heart and body knows it. My spirt knows it. I keep my arms raised in the air, the woman is still talking. I feel my heart beating to the sound of the drums and opening, releasing. Opening, releasing. Tears stream down my cheeks. I am caught off guard. It was never my intention to forgive him. My father died of cancer twenty-eight days before I turned fifteen. Ever since his death and especially since I survived his first assault (whether I knew it or not), I have been on a long healing journey that did not involve forgiving him. For many years I hoped he was suffering somewhere- this man- who caused so much damage and pain to so many. I no longer wished his soul harm but I did not forgive him- until this moment, when the sun and the drums and this ceremony opened my heart. I accept it- forgiveness- and allow it to run through my veins to every part of me, healing, feeding, mending.

From across the universe, her limbs find their way to her torso which has been kept safe, tucked away in a garden in the middle of this big metropolis that is now Mexico City. There, under the brown earth, limbs attach to flesh and the earth nourishes body, healing wounds, healing the emptiness.

A few days after the ceremony at "This Is Not A Cornfield", I am at home, feeling vulnerable from the experience and forgiveness. It is morning and I am getting dressed to go out for the day. I am sitting on the edge of the bed and bend down to put on my shoes. When I raise my upper body, my heart feels like it explodes open. I feel energy emanating from my heart. Light rays pulsing outwards. Instinctively, without thinking, I visualize my son (who is with his father) and my mom (who is with my sister) and see the rays emanating from my heart reaching them. I think of all my loved ones.

One by one, I visualize each of them and see the energy, the light reaching them, healing them. I tear as my heart opens more, the light getting brighter, the rays getting wider. I am in gratitude for this moment, for this healing. I am grateful to be alive. I am grateful to have survived, despite the darkness, the hatred, the utter loneliness and years of depression. I am grateful for my life.

Bathed by the light of the moon, body finds its way to head, attaching, healing, becoming whole as full moon shines brightly in the night sky.

It is early on a Saturday morning and women are gathering for the women's Inipi ceremony in the backyard of a home in East L.A. Linda, host and water pourer, welcomes us as we arrive. At my request, my mother has decided to join me. It is her first time participating in a sweat lodge ceremony. There are about ten women who gather for the ceremony. We begin by helping to cover up the lodge with blankets stored in a nearby shed. The fire keeper has already started the fire in the fire pit, which is few feet from the entrance to the lodge. He carefully adds logs to the flames as white and black smoke swirls up to the sky. We sit on a blanket over the dirt floor to make prayer ties. I help my mom sit on the floor. She is in her seventies and it is hard for her to sit on the ground but she does not complain. She sits next to me and I help her by gathering the materials for her, tobacco and cut out squares of red, black, yellow, green, purple and white cloth. Linda explains the meaning behind the colors used in the prayer ties and shows the women how to make them.

My mom, whose fingers are slightly deformed from arthritis, finds it difficult to place the tobacco in the squares cloths and tie the little bundles to her piece of red yarn. I help her as we listen to the women go around and introduce themselves, speaking about what brought them here today. When it is our turn, I share that coming to Inipi ceremony has helped heal my heart and body. I speak about how much it means to me that my mom has decided to join me, as we both continue on our healing journey.

The ancestors are already gathering around us. Spirit grandmother is here, holding Brendita's hand in hers.

When we are done with the prayer ties, Linda instructs us to form a line as we prepare to enter the lodge. She makes sure that my mom will be sitting close to her, in case she needs to exit the sweat lodge during the ceremony. Before coming in to the lodge, the fire keeper sages us while Linda plays the drum and sings. She has made an altar next to the fire where we may place any items we brought to the ceremony. Linda helps my mom get down to her knees so that she may enter the lodge. Linda explains that we are entering mother earth's womb and this is why we crawl to our spot in the circle, to show our respect and to be closer to the earth. Once inside, Linda asks the fire keeper to bring in any items placed in the altar that will be used in the ceremony. She also asks him to bring in the "grandfathers and grandmothers" or hot lava rocks that have been heating in the fire pit. One of the women receives them using deer antlers to carefully hold and place them in a pile in the middle of the lodge. Linda asks the fire keeper to close the "door" or opening to the lodge. We sit in total darkness and listen to Linda as she prays and sings and then hear the sizzling of water as she pours cold water on the hot grandfathers and grandmothers. I allow the sound of her voice to enter my body, reaching my heart as hot steam and the smell of sweet grass fills my lungs. Beads of sweat blend in with tears as I allow myself to get lost in the darkness, in the steam and the sound of women praying and singing. Knowing my mom is here, praying for our ancestors, for healing, fills me with love and forgiveness for her. I know this is a sacrifice for her. She is Catholic and prays in a very different way than this. I connect to her in the darkness and through her to her mother and her mother before her. I feel all of them here with me. I know they are here too, as we sweat and pray and sing. I know I am not alone anymore.

At that moment, the remaining broken pieces of her heart mend with the whole heart, beating loudly and powerfully in her chest, pumping new blood to her skin and muscles, filling her lungs with oxygen, her body made whole through the power of ceremony, prayer and forgiveness.

Today is Monday August 21, 2017, the day of the "Great American Solar Eclipse" when the total solar eclipse will be seen from coast to coast, across the entire country. My son recently started first grade and is supposed to be in class but his dad and I decided to watch the eclipse with him and take him to school after it ends. We meet at a small park just a block away from my son's school. My son's father and I are not a couple but we share custody of him in an amicable co-parenting relationship. I decide to bring a blanket for us and some of the items from my altar to the park. My son's dad brings special glasses for us to view the eclipse and is open to us having a small ceremony. We are here early, before the eclipse starts. I set the blanket out, which is actually a *zarape*, and bring out items from my altar that I have carefully wrapped for the journey. I place the statute of Coatlicue on a white paisley print bandana that I spread out on the northern side of the blanket. The sky is a bit hazy and the day is already warming up for another hot day in Los Angeles.

I place the two candles I brought next to Coatlicue. They are seven day candles, one is white and the other is red. I place sage, tobacco, a small tin censer, "Open Heart" mist spray, rosary beads, a small disk that depicts Coyolxauhqui, a wooden rattle, a jar of water and a corn husk tobacco cigarette on the white bandana. I also bring out two feathers, one is a hawk feather and the other is a crow feather, which are wrapped in a red paisley print bandana and place them in front of the makeshift altar. I also put out a book titled "Giving Thanks: A Native American Good Morning Prayer," written by Chief Jake Swamp, to read with my son while we wait for the eclipse to start. My son has taken off his shoes and is laying on the zarape. He plays with the special eclipse glasses and is excited to be here.

Coyolxauqui gathers her strength for this battle against brother, against patriarchy. She is whole again. Her ancestors are gathered around her, giving her strength. She is not alone anymore.

The energy of the eclipse is already palpable: a pulsating energy field connecting us to each other, the earth, the trees, the birds and the sky. I use the tobacco to create a circle around us so that we, the *zarape* and the altar are inside the circle. I pray as I do this. I use sage to cleanse us and the space around us. My son wants to use the sage so I hand it to him and he uses it to smudge himself. His dad also takes it and uses it to smudge himself. I put it out on the small censer. There are other people also gathered at the park but they are spread out along the green grass. I use the rattle as I pray. We read the "Giving Thanks" book together and give thanks to Mother Earth, food, the animals and Grandmother Moon. Soon the eclipse starts.

She yells out a battle cry and charges towards him, the bells on her cheeks swinging and ringing with each step. Today she is even more powerful, the most powerful she has ever been, made whole by love and forgiveness and the strength of all those who were raped, beaten and murdered during his reign of terror. She swings her macuahuitl at him, bright rays of sunlight blinding him as they reflect off the dark obsidian blades. He steps back and raises his right arm to shield himself but he is too late. In one forceful swing, she is able to vanquish him, shattering him into hundreds of golden pieces that spread across the blue sky, becoming one with oxygen and light and life.

I play my rattle with one hand and hold the glasses in my other during the eclipse. Through the glasses, the moon appears to be a dark circle equal in size to the sun. It slowly makes its way across the sun, from left to right, small rays of orange and red light crowning the dark circle as the moon completely covers the sun. My heart fills with gratitude for this moment that I am sharing with my son and his father. Soon after the eclipse ends, my son's father leaves to go to work. I stay with my son a bit longer. We sit next to each other on the *zarape*, facing the altar. We speak to each other in Spanish and talk about the energy of the sun and moon. I tell him about their power to heal. I am in gratitude and tell him I am grateful for him. I am grateful that he exists. *Gracias por existir.* I am grateful to be his mother. I thank him for coming into my life.

At that moment her spirit returns to body. Body made whole now. The scars only visible in the sunlight.

As I express my love and gratitude for him, I think of my family members, my friends and loved ones. I think of each of them and send them my love and gratitude. I also send my love and gratitude to our family in Mexico, my cousins, aunts and their offspring. I then think of past generations. I think of my grandmother. I am grateful for her and send her my love. I think of the woman I have been in past lives- the stories I've heard- stories of suffering, beatings and violent deaths and I send them love. I send love and gratitude across the generations, across time. I feel that my heart is a giant ball of energy and that it is reaching across the universe, healing me, healing my son, healing all the men and women who have come before us.

Brendita is here now. She is not alone anymore. Spirit grandmother is here with her. She holds her hand as they stand together. Brendita no longer needs the numbness. She no longer needs the void. She no longer needs the anger or the hatred. She is here now, present in this moment, basking in the love and beaming light of healing.

I hold my son in my arms inside the sweat lodge. This little being that I created, body changing from infant to toddler. Linda prays, evoking our ancestors. Someone is playing the drum, other women sing. My son starts to cry but calms down when I take out my breast and feed him. He is quiet again as we sit in total darkness surrounded by steam and love and medicine. This is his second time in the lodge. He was still in my womb the first time, eight months into my pregnancy. I sit here with my son in my arms, knowing that I will do everything in my power to keep him safe, to make sure that he is not violated. I pray that he knows love, unconditional love. I pray for forgiveness. *Te perdono Brendita.* It was not your fault. I pray for Rosa and Ana. *It was not your fault.* I pray for forgiveness for remaining silent. It was not your fault. I pray for the young woman who hurt her body, cutting, indulging in self-hate. *It was not your fault.* I pray for my body violated again later in life, date raped. *It was not your fault.* I pray for my body, violated yet another time, coerced into sex. *It was not your fault.* I pray for self-forgiveness. You didn't know how vulnerable you were in the hands of other predators. *It was not your fault.*

I pray for her, for myself, for all of us.

Her body is whole again. Coyolxauhqui merges with Brendita, girl child becoming warrior woman, severed wounds healed. Bleeding stopped. Heart is whole again, pumping blood into veins, pumping blood to limbs, feeling feelings again, feeling whole again.

This woman, this dismembered and betrayed woman, made whole through sacrifice, through hard work, through ancestral medicine and healing. She is here now, Brendita, woman now, mother, breastfeeding, praying, healing. Made whole as spirit returns to body. As breast is suckled, as milk nourishes him, her son, her offspring, this next generation, healing, healed. Still healing.

"There is no greater agony than bearing an untold story inside you."

Maya Angelou

Suki Eaton
Mother, Experienced Leader,
Writer, Soulful, Kind,
Essential Being

Suki Eaton is an endearing and spiritual woman whose been coming into her own spiritual gifts. She is wife, mother of two, grandmother of two, a daughter and sister. A native of California, she's attended Mission Junior College and University of Utah Extension for Project Management. She has worked a successful professional career for over 20 years in Management and Administration. She enjoys mentoring people to better themselves, loves nature, the ocean and spending time with her family and friends.

MY SELF-DISCOVERY OF INNER STRENGTH

To the person reading my story, allow me to introduce myself. I am Suki, and I am a Sexual Trauma Warrior. I was abused and attacked from the tender age of 3 to the age of 12. I wish to share my story with you. We each have our personal difficulties in life and all process differently; so don't be afraid to read on because I am a surviving warrior. Here is my story of how I overcame sexual trauma while breaking all the "rules" in a Latino family.

When I was asked about contributing to this book, I was surprised I answered so fast and was shocked at myself. I said yes without thinking about what it really means to me. I never hesitated. I was a bit surprised and honored to be included. Surprised that my story would help someone out in the world and honored to be involved in this band of strong, phenomenal Women Warriors.

Immediately after I committed to adding my contribution to this book, I quickly realized I needed to speak with my parents. I had to think about how I would explain my participation in this book without hurting them in the process because this type of topic was not a common topic anywhere, ESPECIALLY in our culture. In essence, I wanted their blessing to move forward and to show them respect. Both my parents gave me their blessing without hesitation. I really love my parents.

I had a pretty happy childhood for the most part. I am the baby of the family and I am the only girl of three kids. I have two older brothers. They are two and four years older than I. Growing up, I was always told: "You are the Princess" and believed it. My parents are still married, and I don't remember seeing them arguing in front of us often. My mom worked, and my dad stayed home with us. I thought this was normal. I grew up in a typical Latino family in the most Caucasian side of town. This was different than most Latino families as most stayed near each other while raising families.

My dad is the oldest of 17, and my mom is the oldest of 6. Our family was one of two Latino families on the block. Most of my extended family was located in more Latino populated cities. Growing up I never had to face the adversities my parents and grandparents did while growing up or in their young adult years. I like to think our city was progressive for the time and was becoming a cultural melting pot. I also want to mention that I come from a long, **long** line of strong Latina women in my family. Some of the female mentors I have had can crack rocks with one look—that "Latina Mom" look we all fear. Yet, they can be taken down by a child wiser than her young years.

I was often told by my extended family, mainly my cousins, that I was like a coconut. I was brown on the outside but white on the inside. I looked like a Latina but acted white. This was hurtful growing up because it made me feel like I didn't belong in the family. I always felt different and unique. At times I often thought I was just a wallflower observing life, while at other times I felt awkward, like everyone knew my secret.

As I sit back and think of one of my first memories, I often see my family before my grandfather passed over. I remember him like it was yesterday. He was a good grandpa. He would spoil my uncle (the baby of my mom's family), my brothers, and me whenever we were all together. He would take us to the park but not before stopping to buy us lunch. We could have anything we wanted, and he would buy it. Then we'd go to the park to play and to find treasures. He would (without us knowing) throw money in the playground, tell us there were treasures hidden and to go seek them. We would find money, and then he'd take us to the store to buy treats. Life was good. We were always doing something with the family and we still went to visit my grandparents on Sunday.

Then I remember going to the hospital and seeing everyone crying. They wouldn't let us all in at once, so we had to wait for long periods. Then one day we stopped going to the hospital. One of the next memories I have is sitting at church with my cousin and holding a baggie of white powdered donuts. Everyone was sad and we had to be quiet. My great aunt had us sitting next to her, and she kept telling us to be good. We moved from the church to the cemetery. This had a **huge** impact on me. This is where I saw my mom, grandma, and family crying for the first time. I remember they cried the hardest when the coffin was lowered into the ground. I remember at this moment I started to cry. I couldn't understand why, it was too much for my little brain. I could only feel the emotion of my mom and grandma. I don't know who, but someone picked me up and comforted me. I was three years old at the time. I had vivid memories of my life before my grandfather's passing and afterward.

I mention this because not of all my memories were traumatic; which is typically what triggers a reaction. I had many happy recollections as well as some horrific traumatic reminders. My ability to sort became my survival mechanism.

My parents always had visitors at the house. Our house was a landmark house for both sides of my family; it was like Grand Central Station. It wasn't long after my grandfather's passing that I had my first sexual trauma experience. I was around 3 years old. I vividly remember a great-great uncle. He was very old with a wrinkly face and a mustache. He had long, bony fingers and his hands were cold. He wore a cowboy hat and boots. During his attack on me, my parents walked in on him. I cannot exactly recall what happened other than a lot of yelling, but I do remember we never saw him again at the house. The last time I saw him was at his funeral. I believe I was eleven years old when he died. He was just as cold then as when he assaulted me. I remember him as clear as day. I somehow blocked out the attack by my great-great uncle and continued to have a normal childhood for two years.

Then around my fifth birthday, I got a special present from a favorite family uncle, something that would last a lifetime—he assaulted me. He was one of those fun, favorite uncles in the family. He was playful with my uncles, brothers and me. He always included us in games, outside activities and special events. I even remember his wedding. My parents didn't think anything of it when it came to being alone with him. He asked to take me shopping for my birthday. My parents agreed to let me go. We went to Farrell's Ice Cream and then to a toy store to get a gift. He got me a kid version of a black medical doctor's bag. I was really excited. He then took me to his house to "pick up something he left there for my mom."

When we got there, he had me bring in my new toy to play with while he got the "thing" for my mom.

I did as I was told and played in the living room. My uncle then called me to his bedroom and told me he was watching TV and that I should come over to watch with him. I took my toy with me and played on the bed. He started to play with me; I was the doctor and he was the patient. This led to his first attack. I remember crying as it was happening. He told me to stop crying or he would tell my parents I was bad and didn't listen to him, and then they would take my new toy away. I tried to stop crying but it was so painful. I remember the sounds, smells, and terror of my parents finding out I was bad. When it was over, he had me get dressed and snapped at me for not moving fast enough. I was still crying. He never threatened me, nor did he ever talk to me about it. This continued for several years. As a coping mechanism, I learned how to have an out-of-body experience. I withdrew myself from my body as each horrific act took place. I believe this was my way of getting through it. This helped me block out the attacks and move through life like all was normal.

To tell you the truth, I don't know how I learned how to withdraw from my body, but I was so thankful I could do it from an early age. This coping/survival mechanism was what would later keep me from being destructive in my life. I learned how to harness out-of-body experiences throughout my life. I could do it in traumatic times as well as happy times.

I was a good child. I did as I was told and always wanted to please everyone. During the time of being abused by this uncle, I was also abused by several other male family members. All of it was sexual trauma. Just like the other attacks, I would block it out and move on. Each family member who attacked me had their own way of keeping me quiet. This became a way of life for me; I thought it was normal.

I can recall telling and showing an adult what had happened to me. I am guessing that as a child, I didn't know how to tell someone of these attacks, so I showed them what was done to me. It then turned into something that happened a few more times, not initiated by me. As fast as it started it suddenly stopped one day. I believe it was because there was an unexpected knock at the door in the middle of an attack. That made him stop dead in his tracks, never to assault me again.

Several attacks were made by some other male family members who were older than I was but not yet adults. I don't know what made them think I was a person to experiment on. But they did. It never happened for very long. Again, I always knew not to say a word. I hope it stopped because their conscience got the better of them. All these attacks occurred from the age of 5 to 12. I continued using my coping/survival mechanism.

I remember the day I stopped my uncle's attacks on me. I was 12 years old. He was going to take my cousin and me to his company summer party. When he came to pick me up, I had a horrible feeling. I didn't want to go with him, but I wanted to go to the park with my cousin. Before we went to pick her up, we had to go to his house to drop off my bag. We waited for traffic to slow down. He started to touch me again, and it was wrong. I wanted it to stop. I began to scream at him, "YOU'RE MARRIED GO FUCK YOUR WIFE AND NOT ME! LEAVE ME ALONE!" I ran to the bathroom and locked myself in. He then got mad and said we had to leave and we did. I sat in the backseat with my heart beating a million miles a second and felt safe when we arrived at my aunt's house. Upon returning to his home my cousin and I slept in the TV room. I feared he'd come in and get one of us at night. My instincts were correct. He went after my cousin, and I jumped up and yelled at him. He got scared and went to his room. This was also the first time I heard my own voice call out in anger and stand up for myself. As afraid as I was at that moment, I knew I would never allow this to happen again. Life went on. We had family gatherings every weekend, and he was there. He would watch us from afar and never say anything to us.

Earlier, I stated the sexual trauma attacks were a usual way of life for me. Funny how we often don't think of things as abnormal until it's pointed out to us. Then one day, out of the blue, it hit me like a ton of bricks. All these memories flooded my mind. I was emotionally reliving each sexual trauma, each attack, one at a time. I thought I was going crazy. I told my boyfriend that I had been sexually abused as a child. He encouraged me to inform my parents. I couldn't. I felt so much shame. I felt like I somehow deserved it like it was my fault. I didn't know how to cope, or maintain a normal teenage school and family life. I was becoming unglued. I was about to lose all control.

I thought of different ways to tell my parents. *Suicide.* I wrote a note and planned to leave it for when the time was right. This way my parents didn't have to hide the fact that their daughter was a disgrace. The more I thought of doing this I became upset. In the back of my mind, I thought, **Why do these men get to live and hurt someone else and i end my life?** I wanted to make them pay for what they did to me. I wanted everyone to know what they did. I was starting to emerge from that quiet little girl to a vocal young woman.

With the pressure from my boyfriend, I had figured out a way to get the help I needed without harming myself. I thought, instead of writing a suicide letter, I would write to my godmother. She always made time for me, and I respected her. Let me tell you about my godmother. I met her when I was around six years old. She came up with some cousins from Southern California to see one of my other cousins for a visit. I was a shy child around her, but I was attracted to her light. For some strange reason, I wanted to be near her when she was around and sit next to her or hold her hand. She would come up and stay at my parents' house from time to time when visiting my cousins. At one point I asked her for her address. I started to write to her; then it evolved from a phone call here and there into a regular routine. She was kind, and I always felt special when I talked to her. I would even go stay with her when I was visiting from time to time.

When I realized what I had been through, I decided to write her a letter. I always felt I could express myself better in a letter and it felt safer to me. I asked her what she would do if someone she knew was abused or something like that and mailed it. Even though we talked regularly, I was just coming to terms with what had happened to me as a child. I thought this was the best way to inquire and see what she would do or say to me. I was expecting a letter back. Nope, no letter. Instead, I got a phone call—like immediately. This happened to be on a weekend when my parents were out of town. My godmother asked me several questions, to which I answered no. Then she finally asked the question I was dreading and hoping she would ask. She asked me if the letter was about me. I said yes and started to cry. I couldn't think, and I was scared. The sexual abuse was finally out in the open, and there was no going back to the life I knew. She asked me if I was safe. This melted my heart because no one had ever asked me this question before, and at the same time I thought it was an odd question. I felt a bond with her and I knew it would never leave us. I knew right then and there I was going to survive this experience and be a stronger person. My godmother asked me if my parents knew; I said no. She told me I had to tell my mom when she got back from her trip. I told her I would and that I needed a little bit more time after they got back. Deep down I was scared but didn't tell her. I felt I had to be strong and not show any weakness.

She called me the next day when my parents got home. I told her I had not talked to my parents. She said to me if I didn't let my parents know that evening, then she would fly out and tell them with me. I really got scared. I told her I had driver's education that evening but would tell my mom when I got back. She said she was okay with this and would call me the next day to find out how it went and we hung up. Now the pressure was really on me. I knew it was the right thing to do and I was bracing for the response I'd get once I spoke out about my uncle on my mother's side.

I did tell my mom when she picked me up. I said to her that my uncle had sexually abused me. She cried and cried; I cried as well. I told her I thought it was happening to my little cousin and she needed to find out. While she was getting a grip on my news, she called my aunt, and my aunt confirmed it was happening to her daughter as well. My mom told me she needed to tell my father. I said no, she couldn't tell him or my brothers. I couldn't handle the shame. She told me she had to tell my grandmother. I reluctantly agreed, and she called my grandmother. They both cried. I didn't know how to handle this; I was 14 and the last time I saw them crying was at my grandfather's funeral when I was 3. I felt like I was 3 again, but this time no one was there to comfort me and take me away. I never felt as alone as I did that day. I wanted to disappear forever.

True to her word, my godmother called me the next day. I told her about my conversation with my mom, how my aunt confirmed my suspicion about my little cousin, and how the adults talked but nothing happened. I felt in my heart nothing would happen because you don't speak about molestations in a Latino family. **Everyone** knows if you don't talk about it, it didn't happen. I was screaming in my head—**TALK ABOUT IT!!**

Two days after I told my mother, she did tell my dad and family. When my dad found out, he asked me "how do you want your uncle killed?" It was too much for me to answer. My parents asked a few aunts and an uncle to come over to my parents' house to discuss the situation. When my grandmother arrived, she threw a gun and bullets across the table and told me she would kill him. They decided to meet with the uncle in question the next day. I insisted on being there. For some reason unknown to me, this was important. I asked if my little cousin could also be there. They all said yes.

I called my godmother and told her what was going to happen the next day. I was nervous and scared. She calmed me down and told me things would be fine. We drove to my grandmother's house and waited for all to arrive. The uncle in question arrived and was surprised to see me. He asked me what I was doing there. I confronted him and said, "They know what you have done to us." His whole body posture changed. I looked him directly in the eyes and told him again, "They all know what you did to my cousin and me." I kept eye contact with him and my little cousin said, "I hate you, and I don't want you to be my godfather!" I saw the fear in his eyes, and it made me happy. He knew then that the family understood we weren't lying. He then said he would go to counseling to keep the family together. Right then and there, without saying it, he admitted to sexually traumatizing us. That gave me great satisfaction. I was exhausted, mentally and physically.

After a week of nothing happening, I took matters a step further. I talked to a teacher. I knew that by law they are required to report any type of abuse to the police. This would make it real for the first time. It would be out of my family's control. I remember getting a copy of the report and taking it home. My mom was surprised that I reported this to the authorities. Regardless, it was done and real. Reporting this opened the Victim Advocates Programs for my parents and me. We were able to get much needed counseling. After several months of counseling, I was still having a hard time. I wasn't moving forward. I would talk to my best friend from time to time, but it was hard for her to understand. I would also speak to my Godmother. She sensed something still was not right, and she was correct. I had not told my parents about the others who sexually traumatized me. Once that came out, all hell broke loose. The others were close family members. It was a hard time for my parents and me. I had to leave my house at one point and stay with a family friend.

I had a school break coming up. My godmother sent for me. The next thing I knew, I was flying out to Southern California for a week to stay with her. She picked me up from the airport and took me to Laguna Beach. We drove down in her convertible VW Bug with the top down. I barely spoke during the drive to the beach. I just sat with the wind blowing my hair around me soaking up the sun. It felt good not to have to think or talk. I am sure it was a hard drive for my godmother. I was exhausted and wanted not to have to deal with that part of my life. As we approached the beach house, we were sitting in traffic, and out of the blue one of my uncles called out our names and followed us to the house. He wanted to know what was going on and why I was there alone without my parents. I don't know for sure what my Godmother told him, but he ultimately left after a short visit. The week was a much-needed week of healing. It was a week of the beach, me crying and making sense of all that was going on around me. I was protected in Laguna; because of this, the beach will always be our sacred place. I do believe that week saved my life.

At that point, I was in limbo, as to what I would do to myself. My godmother helped me find the light and gave me what I needed, acknowledgment and unconditional love. I finally had validation, and it gave me the strength to be strong and to work through the hardships of my life. After several days of crying, my godmother pulled me out of my funk. She just snapped at me by sternly saying: "That's enough! Now is the time to begin your healing, enough tears." It was shocking at first, but then I knew she was right. I am forever grateful to my Godmother for this time in Laguna. It is amazing how healing the ocean is for me, so much so that I can close my eyes and hear, smell and see it wherever I am in the world.

Upon my return from Southern California, I had a great sense of wanting to be normal. I knew my normal would be different forever. Any child who experienced the things I did at such an early age can never be a child again. I had something sacred taken from me that I would never get back. I was breaking the cultural rules by reporting it to the school. Reporting it to the school started the legal process in motion. My cousin and I didn't have to make a choice to press charges against the predator uncle. The State stepped in and prosecuted him. We did not have to testify against him, and he was indicted and sent to jail; there was justice after all and we were validated legally.

My parents put me in therapy. I will be forever grateful to them for this support. I know many girls don't get therapy. My parents provided it for me, and I was able to work through the many layers of emotional and physical harm. This began an everlasting mental foundation for me. Having access to therapy, I knew I would have the tools in life to be successful.

I would have to rely on these tools throughout my life. One thing I learned was that sexual trauma has a lifelong effect on a person. All I endured would affect me for the rest of my life. At different points in my life I would have to learn to handle the waves of flashbacks. I was unconsciously always on alert.

Earlier in this story, I told you I talked to my parents about this story for their blessing. That part is genuine, but mostly I needed to forgive them. I had a weight on me that honestly I was tired of carrying. I am not going to lie, this was hard for me because I am as stubborn as they come. In my stubbornness, I wanted to hold on to the anger and hurt I endured, and I wanted them to come to me to ask for my forgiveness. As I have reflected on my life, I have realized that I was selfish by holding this over them. I wanted to forgive them now because I have come to terms with the trauma and I have moved on in all aspects but this one area.

My parents are now in their seventies, and I wanted to let them know I forgive them before they pass on to their next journey. I did not want them to pass over to the other side wondering, and I wanted to see them face to face as I forgave them. I asked them to listen to me to hear my perspective on how things happened. I talked to my parents separately and will cherish the conversations forever. As hard as the discussion was, I have no regrets and love them for being open to me. As they listened to me, they had tears and raw emotions. I could see it was eating them up too. We cried, we hugged, and most importantly we talked about it. They validated me. They acknowledged things could have been handled differently, and they told me how proud of me they were for handling it the way I did throughout life. They told me they loved me.

After our conversation it hit me, this would have never happened if I didn't initiate the conversation and how silly of me to wait so long to talk to them. Then I remembered, in our culture, **You do not talk about it. Ever.** I am forever grateful for the opportunity I had to talk to my parents and tell them face-to-face that I forgave them.

Forgiveness, what a powerful and magical thing. It is just a simple word. The mystical influence it has over us is astonishing. Once you say it and mean it, it can move mountains from your heart and clear the air in your head. We all have the power to grant forgiveness. Meaning it is powerful and selfless.

My husband and I will be celebrating our 29th anniversary soon, and I love him more today than I did when we first met. He is solid and my soul partner. We ride the waves of our relationship and marriage. Luckily, we both love the ocean and can ride waves without a problem. I love that he makes me laugh and is so supportive. I want to be a good person for him and our family. We both complement each other, and it's the best thing to show our children and grandchildren. Our daughter moved back to California and is creating her own path. Our son is in the same state as us and has given us two beautiful grandchildren. We are close, and they know I will always be there for them. Even though my husband and I finished raising our children, we aren't ever really done. Our kids continue to amaze me with the good things and all of their life detours. I am proud of our children; I love them and adore them. I know that my husband and

I have given them all the tools to be successful in life. We wish them all the best. I am proud of my family, all the flaws, accomplishments and memories.

My wish for you is to see your inner light and to know you are not alone. Others have had similar experiences and will be there to support you when you choose to come forward. Remember, there is a light at the end of the tunnel. Just reach out to it. You are worth the effort and it's time to be validated. I believe you and want you to know for all you have endured, you are stronger than you think, and you have the power to heal your wounds.

I am so proud and thankful to be a part of this book and group. There is mystical energy within these pages. These women warriors have all banded together to uplift the women of our culture and other cultures. We have all taken a stand to share the unspeakable, to help validate you and all you have endured.

I have a blessed life. I had the strength to overcome my sexual trauma. I have made a beautiful family unit, and I love them. I became a confident, respected and happy woman in my personal and professional life. Thank you for allowing me to show you how it is possible to grow from a traumatic experience. Working hard and making a difference in this life is a choice. I will now pass on my strength, passion and inner warrior to you and future generations to come. Many blessings to you during your journey. Amen and Yo También!

"Do what you feel in your heart to be right -for you'll be criticized anyway."

Eleanor Roosevelt

Gena Contreras
Mother, Activist, Empath, Holistic Healer Specializing in Essential Oils and Nutrition, Spiritual Being.

Gena has over two decades of experience in management, customer service, and sales. Her creativity has also helped her become a talented make-up artist and a chef. She is an expert on healthy holistic living with the proper use of essential oils and creating blends to help harmonize the mind, body, and spirit. Her most treasured role in her life is a Mother to her four beautiful children. The love of her family is the fuel which supports all of the work she does.

WARRIOR MOTHER

I arrived in the winter of 1969, born only 18 months after my eldest brother in Los Angeles California. Both my parents are of Mexican-American descent. My father enlisted in the Marine Corp at 19, months before I was born. I cannot even imagine what went through his consciousness knowing he could perish like so many young men. Then I think of her, my mother, alone during this scary time having two babies under the age of two. What went through her mind? Could she be thinking of her children not having a father? Was she distraught by his absence or could she be feeling trapped and alone? I spoke with her years later as I researched my childhood, and she shared her resentment. She said he left her pregnant with a baby. She resented him for years due to his decision. They were young and completely disconnected from each other. Their marriage suffered profoundly. Bitterness and lack of respect consumed their 22-month nuptials.

My father came back definitely a different man, no longer a boy, he was a Marine. One with stories of vivid images of war. What he witnessed and endured, gives you goosebumps. One story I can recall is having most of his bunker killed by the enemies due to one sergeant falling asleep during his watch. He lost serviceman daily. The result of this uncertain time of war is deep scars, post traumatic stress disorder (PTSD) and multiple surgeries on his lower back. What drove him to leave us is a question that might never be answered. Was he running from his own fears? Or did he have a profound need to accomplish something admirable and honorable as a young man? This is his story to tell.

My parents each remarried, and I mostly stayed with my mom and stepfather, visiting my father on weekends. My family dynamic was unique and complicated; I had a stepsister my age, a younger half-sister my mom had with my stepfather, a half-brother my father had with my stepmother and my own brother. This was always a fun explanation to those questioning our relationship. It's like the phrase "His, Hers and Ours." Yet, I loved all my siblings the same. They were my brothers and sisters. My stepsister and I were only six months apart, so at times many thought we were twins. My mother had an extraordinary connection to my brother, possibly because he is her first born. My stepsister had a deep-rooted bond with my stepmother that no one could come between. Then there was me, the questionable child. I always felt less loved throughout my childhood, suffering the middle child syndrome in both homes. The reason was due to an intimate conversation with my father. He told me when my mother became pregnant unexpectedly, nine months after my brother- she was not ready for two babies so close in age. She contemplated the idea of having an abortion to ease herself from being a mother of two young babies. At the time of this conversation, my spirit felt unwanted and unloved.

My relationship with my mother was never good. It wasn't loving or understanding. I was a unwanted child coming into this world and it haunted my existence. My mother endured physical and emotional abuse, which understandably is why the cycle of abuse reached me. She coped by drinking possibly to numb and suppress her own sadness and pain. As a young child, I looked at her and thought how captivating she was. I would write poems and notes usually using an old typewriter in my stepfather's office; there I found a way to create words of love and kindness. I would burn the edges of the paper to create a vintage marking. I would place the notes on her vanity while she got ready for her day. My intention, as a young child was to validate the importance of her existence. I wanted to show her how much she was loved and admired as if my young spirit perceived her pain. I needed her to see me and love me. I often wondered how children can love unconditionally with so much of themselves; their love is pure with no judgment. This profound understanding became clear to me as I became a mother. Knowing my children will love and look at me with the same unconditional love, made me accountable for my actions.

Then came the visits to my father's new home. It was a white 1930's home with a huge attic later restored as my bedroom. There were two eerie, beautiful large trees on each side of the home, great for climbing out of the attic window when needed. The backyard was huge. There was an old garage we used mainly for storage. Being young and unfamiliar in my new home, I always asked if I could get snacks from the refrigerator. As long as we ate our meals we were allowed to snack. Fridays were especially fun, we kids could treat ourselves to candy or possibly a soda. It wasn't often we had junk food to eat.

My father was a stern, powerful military man. I did my very best never to cross him. He had a strong voice that can shake your soul. Any kid he coached could explain the capabilities of his voice. He was adored and respected for taking kids off the street to play ball. Teaching them the importance of respect and hard work. Belt out if anyone of us lied. One child lied, we all suffered the consequences.

Lining us all up waiting for the terror of his hand or the belt to our backsides. I remember it being my turn never crying, as much as it hurt, knowing I didn't lie. I wasn't going to show him my weakness nor was he going to break me for something I didn't do. The more he spanked me, the more he was defeated. My brother and sister cursed me for the frustrations he would take out on them. He will always be the first teacher in my life. He became the man who would mold me into a strong, hardworking woman with integrity and profound respect in all my dealings through life. His strong upbringing gave me the lesson that perfection and respect are admirable. Own your promises and never show weakness.

My brother and I were instructed to call our new stepmother, 'mom.' This very broken woman was tight-fisted behind closed doors and said unimaginable words to me about my mother. She spoke as if I was her. I felt at times I was cursed for being the child of a man she was obsessed with. Calling me names like "whore," "bitch", "stupid" and *"cabrona"*- basically, the same as being called a bitch in Spanish. Being locked in the dark attic when she casted me away, only confirmed my feeling of being unloved and invisible. This confused me at such a young age. I felt as if she knew my soon to be predicament with sexual abuse.

She was fiery, with red long hair and nails, dressed immaculately and could dismiss you away with a glare. She so loved my father and became obsessed pleasing him. We were being groomed and becoming slaves in our own home. Our job was to ease the living environment for my father. Immaculate house; yard raked and watered; every leaf picked out of the sparkly white rocks that landscaped the front porch; and screens cleaned monthly due to heavy dust from so much dirt. We massaged his feet or back when he was feeling depleted. Father's Day and his birthday were like Christmas, gifts wrapped up beautifully; all for her man, our father. Of course there were good memories. Unfortunately, the bad outweighed the good. Each parent spoke ill of the other, and I would go back and forth from one home to the other. Exhausted, caught in the middle, stressed, listening and living in all this turmoil, my spirit slowly becoming undone by the physical and emotional abuse I experienced in each home. To lessen the tension and my constant fear, I learned to anticipate what each parent needed from me before they could ask. I learned to be perfect. I learned to be invisible.

I was four years old and already doing things on my own, I learned to do my own hair, ironed my clothes and laid them out the night prior to school. Cleaning was my forte; having two meticulous mothers gave me a foundation of accomplishing my chores. To feel important and with a purpose, cleaning quickly gratified me. I mastered it. I can enter any room and recognize displacement. It became an obsession. I had to do it. My home life was broken in every sense of the word. I felt a sense of control with my new passion. I loved playing with my dolls, Barbie's preferably. I can still do my eyeliner like them. I dressed them beautifully, their life was perfect. Boats, RV's, swimming pools, etc. They had so many friends, and their perfection enchanted me. When you are perfect, your untouchable, invincible and still. No one can or should harm you. So all my dolls had their own place on the shelf. I organized all their shoes and accessories. My room was always in order, especially at my father's house.

Our beds had to be smooth, wrinkle-free and taut. Structure was an understatement.

During my time with my mom, having company over was the social thing to do in the 70's. No social media or cell phones. Company came over unannounced with alcoholic beverages and some good conversation. Unfortunately, there were a few friends and family members that misbehaved. Some would get intoxicated and not mind their manners. That is when the unspeakable happened. My mother's brother would come over to watch us, while parties were taking place. He was a teenager developing into his own manhood and I was a little girl trying not to disrupt my parent's world. We had many conversations, and I trusted him. He made me feel like I was important. I remember the green drapes closed, the beige carpet, the 70's bedding, the musty, musky smell of the room and of him. To an innocent four-year-old, I thought it was normal to be touched that way. He had conditioned and groomed me to feel good, and I was quick to acknowledge that being touched this way was a form of love. Something I have not felt. Lost was the innocence that a four-year-old should never lose. In place of my lost innocence was this convoluted and corrupted sense of love. For the longest time in my relationships with men, this haunted and confused me. While writing my story, I remembered the unfortunate situation of my young self and the awful experience my body endured. No child should ever suffer the way I have. I would find baby photos of myself and apologize to that little girl. How did I survive all I endured as a child? It made me stronger and a true empathetic individual. Through all my dealings with individuals, I learned never to judge another. To always love unconditionally.

As I write my story, I have been able to sit down with family members and ask them to share their story. It makes me feel like I can tell my own story and start a conversation. I know deep in my heart this amazing book will be a new beginning for them and for their families, allowing recovery to be their foundation.

My stepfather was my safe place. The one parental figure that made me feel protected and seen. Our relationship was everything I longed for with my own father. He too was a military man, who married my mother after his service in the army. He listened and guided me. The constant negativity in both homes was inescapable, but I found order in the challenge of schoolwork and chores.

I was self-sufficient and survived by being still and quiet. It meant being untouched. I thought it could shield me from any type of abuse that came my way. My stepfather seemed to always know my heart and how it was broken. I was always hiding from my mother's scolding ways. I once hid in a wicker laundry basket all day, knowing my mother was trying to find me after she discovered I accidentally threw a rock across the street and broke a man's window. My stepfather found me and diffused the situation by explaining to my mother that it was purely an accident. I loved him for protecting me. In their marriage I saw the most distressing situations - it shook my spirit. Their fights were alarming, and I sometimes ran next door to hide when my mother was drinking and misbehaving, knowing I would be caught up in her wrath. I loathed those days; I never understood the quick unexpected slaps that startled me. I wasn't safe nor did I want to be anywhere near her. My heart broke once I learned my mom and stepfather were getting a divorce.

At times I blamed myself because I was so fond of him and felt possibly she resented me for it.

By the time I was 10, my parents had an ugly custody battle. My stepfather and mother divorced. My brother and I now permanently lived with our father. Signs of depression were manifesting from my secret and silence about what happened to me at age four after losing my stepfather. I thought I could survive with an exterior of perfection. I stopped eating. I wanted to die and be gone. For twenty-four days I starved myself. I lost control of everything around me, all I had was my physical being. My soul and spirit were torn and shredded. My whole self was completely compromised. Then, my father saw how gaunt I was. I'd hide with layering clothes trying not to be seen. The exposed ribs, the dark circles, the cry for help, silently took over. Still silent, I continued this cruel self sabotage. I was placed on medication without inquiry. If they did ask, I couldn't hear anything. I could only hear my cries of deep traumas. So I continued this punishment of my body. It gave me sick gratification, control and eased my inner pain. I needed to take back something of my own. That was my relationship with food, as detrimental as it was. It was mine! For years, this relationship consumed me. I had to seek professional help so I could learn that food is meant for thriving and fueling the body.

At 18, I ran away from home to live with my aunt. Without knowing it, I was approaching a confrontation with my four-year-old self. I had a boyfriend, whom I loved, and our relationship embodied so much about what I knew about love; it was violent. He was an alcoholic, and I expressed my rage silently with an eating disorder.

There was a very handsome neighbor living across the street, a police academy trainee, who seemed like a decent guy. We exchanged hellos, he came over a few times, and we talked. My attraction to the neighbor was never more than a casual friendship. Then one afternoon, after my boyfriend had dropped me off at my aunt's house from being at the beach, my neighbor walked into the house, uninvited. I heard someone come in, but before I could even ask what he was doing there, he grabbed my shoulder and turned my face down into the bed. I was wearing only a long T-shirt and my bathing suit. My face was in the pillow, and I couldn't breathe, he pulled down my bottoms and raped me in a place a woman should never experience. I was on my stomach, trying to fight back, kicking him, trying to grab him with the one hand he didn't have pinned down. It seemed like forever. Finally, he was done. I was hyperventilating as he walked away. I was unable to talk. What just happened to me? Was this my fault!? I felt like the little girl I was at four years old, stolen innocence and ashamed. Not perfect or in control. The neighbor walked back into the living room and left me in pain.

My boyfriend returned because he told me he didn't have a good feeling when he saw the neighbor starting to walk over as he left. He walked straight into the room I was in, I pointed toward the door while I cried. He beat the neighbor with his fists, black and blue, the neighbor walked out dumbfounded. I remember my boyfriend asked me what I did so this person felt he could just come in without an invition. That moment I questioned myself. Am I an awful girl? I went to school dumbstruck, a teacher I trusted approached me, and I told her of the incident during the weekend. Next thing I was at the hospital and made a police report. I remember being in these stirrups at the doctor's office as my examination continued. To this day, I have anxiety while being vulnerable in this position. The conclusion was interal physical trauma. Is that even possible? To have trauma inside your body? It's not like your spirit or soul being traumatized, it is now physical in a place I would never imagine. Now, every part of me is jaded. The scars I carry that no one could see. Yet the sone thing I did well was pretend to be perfect on the outside. Speak to others with compassion and understanding. Do well at school and always shield myself from everyone.

I moved back to my father's house, trying to keep yet another secret from my parents to no avail. The investigator calling regularly and my aunt told them of the rape. Just like that, I felt backed into a corner. I couldn't make this go away. I had to tell my father I wasn't so innocent or perfect. I was broken, having no idea about how to place the pieces back together perfectly. That's when my fourteen-year-old secret I hadtried so hard to bury surfaced. I told them everything. I remember being so numb yet strong. I told them who it was when it happened, everything. For the first time, I felt real empathy from my parents. I felt safe with them. It was such a wonderful feeling to be seen by them for what seemed like the first time. It was the start of healing to finally unburden myself, but with still so much self-blame. I never went through with the arrest of the neighbor because I wasn't ready to face the repercussions that come with being the victim. For years, I lived with the thought that I allowed this person to get away with traumatizing my body and soul and maybe someone else's body and soul too. It took me years to forgive myself. To understand it was my only way of surviving. Now that the family knows and knows the perpetrator, how can the family delude their emotions? I often wondered how families can allow these detestable people to be around children as if it was normal. Many families live in denial not to correct the issues that seem to be hindering and destroying the spirits of our children. They have no voice. I cannot even imagine having children and allowing them to suffer, is why I told myself I'd never bring them into this destructive world, but I will always be a voice for the children of the world.

At 19, I ran away with a man to Ojai, an enchanting town in the Valley of Ventura County, California. For the first time, I felt free from negativity. My soon to be mother-in-law became my second teacher in life. She owned an amazing health food store where I was able to work. I learned to create beautiful, healthy sandwiches and salads in the kitchen. We made soups everyday. Juiced only the freshest fruits and vegetables in a juicer. I was captivated and enthralled. Never had my passions run wild. I am being schooled daily on nutrition and healing through food. I learned about spirituality and homeopathy. Everything about this place gave me a new perception of my life. It was all so new and exciting. She saw I was dealing with depression and offered me some supplements and a book on sugar. I'll never forget that book, "Sugar Blues." This book opened my eyes to how sugar is more addictive than heroin; it was the culprit in many ailments and discomforts of the body, especially the mind. I was like a sponge, able to quickly absorb every lesson and conversation.

Not soon after I realized I couldn't label myself as a victim. I now had to work through my pain. Months later

I became pregnant, and my then boyfriend wanted to get married. I wasn't sure, everything was happening too quickly, yet I knew I couldn't have the baby unwed. I thought only of my grandmother's request, so off we went with my boyfriend's family to Las Vegas to get hitched. I remember very clearly the tugging of my heart, my mother did not take the time to see me, nor could I speak to my father since I ran away. I was all alone and feeling unloved once again. In Vegas, I began having heavy cramping, something was going on. I was bleeding. The night before my wedding I lay lifeless in a strange hospital losing my baby, losing blood. Laying in the hallway unconscious due to lack of available rooms,. The doctors were scared I had lost too much blood. I came to and my soon-to-be family took me back to the hotel. I awoke ready to say, "I do," without thinking about what had just happened to me physically. I did not want to disappoint. I got up and dressed and left to the chapel where my grandparents surprised me. I was elated, and tears fell down my face. My loves were there for me. At the time, my grandfather suffered from diabetes and lost most of his eyesight, yet he managed to walk me down the aisle as I held his hand and guided him. The most profound moment of my life. I was now married.

The pain from my own childhood was very clear in my interactions in my new marriage. Two years after my miscarriage, I became a mother to my first child, a son. Three and a half years later, I would have my daughter. They were my will to live; these precious souls who allowed me to feel a love I could not comprehend. A love that melted my heart every moment with them. All I knew is that I must protect and nourish my children. I implemented every teaching my mother-in-law taught.

Rarely, when they became ill, I used only homeopathic remedies to ease a fever or comfort a cough. I learned at those moments that I was their healer. I placed my hands over their bodies and spoke to their spirits. I would say to them, 'tell your spirit to get better.' I used my intuition. I know that the mind and spirit of healing go hand in hand. This never did this failed me.

During this time, though, my marriage was becoming more turbulent and violent. I came to the realization that I placed myself in the same environment I was in as a young child. All the pain from my own childhood surfaced in my marriage, my depression was heavy, we were young, and the cycles of abuse in both of our families, the patterns of dysfunction and toxicity were repeating themselves. I had to learn to make things right and heal; I just couldn't do it with this man. It became a chore to love; I was a prisoner in my own home. The only happiness and smiles I had, came from my children. I was now teaching my children about self-love, and the boundaries of their own bodies; the color of their beautiful dark skin; how to love unconditionally; how to speak to people; and how to respect others. As a mother, I became a woman of purpose. I had to teach my children to be completely happy and safe. I thought of my own self, and I made a promise to never allow my children to experience the ugliness of sexual trauma. I became a damn great protector! No one will hurt them as long as I'm breathing. I struggled in this marriage for nine years until I had had enough and needed to end my marriage. How I ended my marriage cost me a profound lesson, I am not proud of what I did, yet I knew I had to get out before I became a ghost.

Still, the decision to leave was difficult. I left with the shirt on my back and started from ground zero. It was time to stand on my own two feet and be brave. I found work in customer service, worked for amazing companies where I felt empowered and understood my self-worth. Working in customer service was perfect for me; it was a foundation of extending my deep love of hospitality. I saved money and got my first apartment. It was so gratifying, these accomplishments, they gave me the encouragement to keep moving forward. I wanted to keep the courts out and avoid a custody battle. I could not have done to my kids, what was done to me.

My children were now from a broken home, but I needed them to understand that my choices were about survival, because I wanted them to be safe, protected and well loved. Although I had the courage to leave, I still wasn't giving myself the love I needed. I had yet to learn how to protect myself from men. I allowed my ex-husband to control a lot of the decisions about our children, as we learned how to navigate co-parenting. It took me quite some time to learn how to protect myself from his wrath. He was vocal and screamed straight through my inner child, crucified me with daggers, and I often felt exhausted of our quarrels.

Once I was strong, I realized he was a tyrant. I had to remember I had a responsibility to go up against him with love and compassion. Once I did that, he was able to speak to me like an adult. I learned a communication style I had not had with my own parents. I stopped myself from being afraid to mend our relationship for our children's sake. I placed my children before my selfishness. Life became tolerable after too many years of resentment. I looked at my own broken marriage to this man as if I was mending my own parent's marriage. Once we began our journey keeping our children first, we began to apologize to one another, for the pain and destruction we started. Walking side by side, we finally accomplished a healthy partnership, for the sake of our children as for ourselves.

I began to have faith. Although I was raised Catholic, I never really believed in anything, and yet I began to pray. Christianity moved me; the realization something powerful and benevolent is watching and protecting me, shaping my inner beauty. I started to forgive my abusers and myself, and I prayed for all of us. Deep emotions were surfacing and being released. It was a real turning point for my children and myself.

During this time alone with two children, working towards a better future. I met an amazing man that was quite younger than I. He loved me unconditionally, and I bared every pain, trauma, and heartbreak from my past to show him who I truly was. I was curious to see if he wanted to be with a woman who had been broken and did her best to fit the pieces back together. He accepted me! He was a source of contentment, and I was giving and trusting of his love. Could this be the one? I always knew he was. Keeping my faith and prayers loud, I began to grow and blossom as a woman. He made me feel important and safe. Our relationship seemed so flawless and easy.

Soon after, I was blessed with a baby boy I named Moses. Never thought I'd have any more children after losing my right ovary in an unforeseen accident. I called him my miracle baby, his little face looked like a doll, he was perfect, and now I get to raise him with a man who loves us both. As I matured, I remember a prayer I had at 19, I had asked God to bless me with a baby to love and protect but I lost that child traumatically. I thought of this spirit many times throughout my life, and on my 38th birthday I made a wish, I wanted one more child. He answered my prayers months later, and Joshua Mychal arrived in the summer of 2008.

I'll never forget the moment he started to speak, he would tell me of his life before me, he would fly through the sky looking all over for me. I was amazed and speechless as he told me stories about before he was born. I thought, could this be the baby I lost 20 years ago? He said he looked all over for me in the heavens. "I had to find you, and I chose you to be my mommy," My spirit fluttered, this is not something a typical 3-year-old would say. At this time I knew he was the little spirit I lost 20 years prior. He now found his home, and he is the image of me. What an amazing gift. I think back of the little girl who fought to survive, the one with all the bad luck. I sometimes cannot believe I am writing my story, sharing it with so many other women just like me. In moments when I reflect on my trauma, I remember that I would close my eyes and tell myself, tomorrow is a new day, the sun will shine, and this is only temporary. I will be in bed soon to rest and dream beautiful dreams of my life. I smile when I think of that. So for those still struggling, know there is beauty in this world. We can create our own safe, beautiful spaces. They belong to us.

> *"When you're enduring pain, visualize, tomorrow is a new day, the sun will shine, and this is only temporary."*
> - Gena Contreras

I will always grow as most of us do; yet I now have molded and fine-tuned these upsets into beautiful paintings on the horizon of my life. Through my life of much turmoil and my unfortunate family cycles of abuse, I made extraordinary leaps and choices for my children and myself. I am still standing. Never will I forget where I came from; to always help broken women; and, offer the story of my past to encourage those that need uplifting.

I am a strong role model and I work as a humanitarian for the children of the world. I'm an activist for transparency; I fight laws that hinder our parental medical freedoms. It's a profound fight, but worth saving babies. That is another story in itself. In 2012, I was diagnosed with a disorder called fibromyalgia. It's a complex disorder even doctors can't seem to pinpoint the cause. It's taken me down as far as being bedridden for months. The pain is like having worked out for hours, the fatigue is by far the worst. It devours your whole being. Healing oneself has been one of the most important pieces of my life. Having this disorder has opened up much of my own childhood trauma, allowing me to go in deep and heal.

When I was asked to write my story, I had just moved back to Los Angeles with my father after running away at 19. This emotional return has me delving deep into all that you read in my story. I call it a divine intervention. Only I can heal myself by facing my ultimate fears. I am realizing my condition as that of many women; we must stand in unity, help one another and speak to each other. That is when our healing begins. We find the root of our pain and start to clean out the old memories; maintain our own bodies and nourish it back to life. Helping women and mothers with natural remedies for healing has earned me a placement in society. I am giving a piece of my own education to those that can benefit. It's been a true testament that has brought so much happiness. I now consider myself a warrior for our children and for our women of the future.

"Change the way you look at things and the things you look at change."

Wayne Dyer

Chella Diaz
Author, Intuitive Life Coach, Energy Healer, Mother, Transcend Abundance Workshop Facilitator

Chella knew at a very young age she was different from the other kids. She was able to see and feel things other kids could not. She didn't want to stand out so she put her gifts to sleep. She was married for 17 years and has two sons. For over 10 years, Chella has been on her spiritual journey.

The list of certifications and programs she has completed is quite extensive but to include a few Reiki Master, Starlight Energy and her most recent which brought all her certifications together in a powerful way 7th Dimension Healing Energy.

HIDING IN PLAIN SIGHT

There are such fond memories of my early years as a child. I was filled with joy and delight. I would laugh and smile all the time. Loving the outdoors; chasing butterflies, playing marbles with my brothers and friends, and enjoying all the world had to offer me. Each day was a new journey for my young mind. I longed to know how things worked. Watching others for not only guidance, but for the explanation of why things are the way they are. Like any young girl I wanted to know why the sky was such a vivid blue and what made the grass such a deep emerald shade of green. Starved for knowledge I would seek understanding by asking questions and observing for comprehension to all there was to learn.

One of the things I enjoyed most of all was going to the fruit and vegetable stand in the *mercado*. I would stand at the entrance to the marketplace taking in all the sights, sounds and smells of the different vendor booths and crowd around them. First I would look to see who had the biggest, ripest tomatoes and begin my shopping. The produce stands seemed so big then. I couldn't hand the money over the counter because I was so young and small at the time. So with no fear I would go into the stand next to the mountain of fruits and vegetable and pay. My parents would leave the money for me in a jar on our kitchen table. I would always have a few coins left over that I could save giving me a sense of the value of money which would later lead to helping me purchase my first car at 17 years old.

One thing I did earlier on with the money I had saved and other money I made doing chores around my neighborhood was show some boldness as an eager eight year old. I had always had long hair. My father was very traditional and believed girls should have long hair. I had wanted my hair cut short. After all it was the "sixties" and those short pixie and Peter Pan cuts were so cute. I took my hard earned coins to the beauty shop and got my hair cut. Thinking back I'm sure I had nowhere near enough money to pay for the cut, and most likely my parents did make up the difference. But I was proud of myself and felt like a rebel.

For as far back as I could remember I felt a sense of adventure, curiosity and even a little defiance up until...

When I was nine years old my family, that consisted of my parents, my two younger brothers and myself, lived in Juchitlan, a small town outside of Guadalajara. In the spring of that year my mother and father had made arrangements for us to move to the United States. Time had come to start getting ready for the move. We were going to be leaving soon and needed to start packing and move things to my grandmother's house where we would be staying until we were ready to leave. Living in a small community with many of our relatives nearby, my brothers were sent to stay with one of my aunts in order to be out of the way while my parents and other family members and I were packing. There were five adults at our house going back and forth to and from my grandmother's place.

It was about 7:00 p.m. when I was told to go to bed. I slipped on my comfy flannel, oversized, nightshirt and did as I was told. It had started to rain. I could hear the pitter-patter of drops on the roof, which was a pleasant sound and made me relax getting ready to sleep. The smell of the rain on the dirt came through the window. It was a musty smell of wet clay.

Not long after I went to bed all of the adults were taking things to the other house. For some reason my uncle, who I will call Tio Chango, came back to our house and ended up alone with me in my room. Why wouldn't he come back to the house; it made sense my parents were at the other place delivering the stuff and Tio Chango was at our house getting something else to take to the other house. He came into my room and sat on the side of the bed. I didn't know why he was sitting with me until he started touching my private area with his hand. Although I was young I could tell he was getting pleasure. I had no idea what was going on. My body stiffened. The lower half of my body had a sensation of burning and then becoming numb. His touch was sickening, nauseating, revolting. I felt queasy and my stomach was in pain like I had been punched. I will never forget the feel of his hands on me. The roughness of his calluses and the satisfaction he gave himself from doing this to me. As I write this I am reminded of and can still see the look in his eyes and how scared I felt. That smell of wet clay, even so many years later, actually decades later, makes me so sick to my stomach and causes a visceral reaction in my body.

The whole encounter took place over about ten minutes. There were people coming back from grandmother's house and so he stopped. He gave me that look in his eyes again and held his index finger up to his lips, "Shhh" I was terrified. He came back later and asked me if he could do it again. I could not speak I was in such shock. Why had this happened to me? I was nine years old.

Where were my parents in all this? This man was my family he should be protecting me, not molesting me. I became lost and lived in fear of this secret that night and felt as though I would never recover from it.

In the following days two men in their twenties, that were neighbors, attempted to touch and hold me. I ran away as fast I could; so much so that when I got home my mother thought I was running a race. I never told anyone!!! How did they know what had happened to me with Tio Chango that they thought it was alright to try and touch me as well. For years I thought there was some way to tell just by looking at me that I was someone that could be used and abused at anyone's whim. Like a target or sign was on my forehead. How could my mother and father not know what was happening to me?

We eventually moved to the United States to Venice, California. It took a couple of weeks to drive there. I went about my life and buried the emotions of my assault from Tio Chango.

I hid myself at Broadway Elementary in Venice, CA by learning English and participating in all the American and Mexican holidays. I was part of a Mexican dance group at school. I thought I would like this, however most of the dance teachers were men which made me uncomfortable. I remember not wanting to spend much time with men. I was always afraid the men I was around would know about what had happened to me with Tio Chango and think they could and would take advantage of me. Again I would spend time thinking about where were my parents when Tio Chango touched me.

I started middle school at Mark Twain in Venice, California. When I was in the sixth grade, I had to walk a long way to get there. The black students used the school buses. At the time nonblack students would get beat up if they got on the bus. So I kept mostly to myself and found it better to take the long walk. I eventually made a few friends, but I was shy and afraid people would find out what happened to me with Tio Chango. I was in a complete shell and would not open up to anyone. I was doing my best to hide in plain sight. Two years after our move to Venice Tio Chango came to California to live nearby.

I always went to summer school so I could fill up my days. I was a good student and received awards and honors during my time there. Perfect attendance, good citizenship awards, and hallway monitor to name a few prior to graduation.

While I was in middle school my dad worked two jobs for about six months; one of the paychecks went into an account for a down payment on a house and the other was for our living expenses. I graduated, and during the summer between middle school and high school my dad bought a house and we moved to Carson, CA. The move was not easy for me as I left behind the couple of friends I had made. My father would take me to visit them occasionally for about a year afterwards, but as it happens we did finally lose touch with each other.

In high school, the badminton coach saw potential in me and asked me to join the team. I was excited about this because I knew it would take up time outside of school and fill up more of my days. I got to compete and go to other schools. I started to feel good about myself.

I enjoyed competing and going to other schools where I was allowed to interact with other students. My mother was a little upset about me being on the team because it gave me less time for chores. We lived in Carson for 3 years. My dad sold the house and purchased a 6-unit property in Lennox the summer prior to my senior year. I will say I was disappointed not to be able to compete on the badminton team any more.

In high school, during one of the sex education classes I learned, really for the first time that is not okay for anyone to touch your private area regardless of the relationship. Once this idea had come up to me again, I started to withhold from people, and kept to myself. I went deeper into my shell. I was afraid people would find out about my secret.

My parents were traditional and conservative. They did not allow me to go to friends, house or parties. The only type of parties I knew of were family gatherings where people would get drunk and eat a lot. Many of the family parties were in large dance halls with live bands, and yes you guessed it, there was always an adult with us. In addition, I was not allowed to date. I remember thinking how am I going to find a husband if I cannot date.

During my senior year in high school, I was going to two different high schools. I attended Lenox High School and also took classes in Hawthorne. As a result I had no roots and didn't make friends. This actually worked for me as I was able to stay in my shell and not be noticed since I didn't belong in either place. I was permitted to work at "Pup N Taco". I was very naïve and I didn't understand some of the jokes the other employees thought were funny. To this day I don't get a lot of the jokes; it's not my thing. I especially don't appreciate jokes made at the expense of others. This still kept me in my shell and from making new friends. However, this job allowed me buy my first car.

After high school I was given an opportunity to do an air force internship for three months. My father had told me I needed to get a paying job. For the first time since my eight-year-old self had cut her hair I stood up to my father and told him I wanted to do the internship instead and did. That little rebel was starting to show her head to find her way back. Not only the rebel but the part of me that was curious and wanted to know things about the world. The air force seemed like a place for this to happen. After all it was only for three months. I worked with a wonderful woman who took me under her wing so to speak and gave me a wealth of knowledge in a very short time. Later I would go to work for her again in a paying job. When I finished my internship I attended Santa Monica College and studied communications. I later went to L.A. Trade College.

When I was twenty years old I was working full time at a lending office and I often had to go to the bank to make the deposits. I had gotten acquainted with a nice lady at the bank, Jennie, and she invited me to a Kool and the Gang concert. The day of the concert we met at her house and drove from there to the event. As we were leaving I met her younger brother, he seemed like a nice guy. Jennie and I became good friends and she invited me to her house for Thanksgiving dinner. We didn't celebrate Thanksgiving in my family. Jennie had wanted to set me up with her older brother, but when I got to her place for dinner her older brother was not home. He had gone out so I got to know her younger brother instead. He asked me out and although I thought he was a bit too tall I decided I would go out with him. On a side note, a few weeks prior I had met two different guys that said they would call me at a certain time and didn't. So I made up my mind I would not wait by the landline forever for Jennie's brother to call. I know I am dating myself, cell phones were not around at the time. So if he didn't call at the time he said he would I was not going to wait. Well, he called right on time and we went on our first date. We saw each other every day for about one month. Four months later I moved in with him.

In a very short time we had our first son, we got married and had our second son. I had a full time job at a lending office and volunteered at the PTA; I wanted to be an involved parent. One of my favorite memories is when I organized a Cinco De Mayo dance. I reached out to family and friends to help with the food. I was a bit concerned about how many people were going to show up so I used alcohol to bribe a few friends to come to the dance. I made margaritas for them. Yum. One of my friends was afraid she was going to get caught drinking on school grounds. Oh heavens those were some fun times. Another wonderful recollection is that I also played paddle tennis twice a week to release stress. As you can tell I kept myself busy. I wanted to be a good mom, attentive wife and excellent employee.

After I gave birth to my second son I could not release the weight no matter what diet or exercise program I did. I went to have my tubes tied and I while they were doing the surgery they found a terrible infection which would have prevented me from having any more kids. Looking back, I now know that it was by body protecting itself from not wanting to be touched inappropriately.

My sons were very active in sports and we were always on the road. Every holiday weekend we would spend at a sporting event.- basketball, football, water polo, and swimming.

Fourteen years into my marriage, my mother-in-law passed away and life as I knew it was over. She had lived on the east coast, and I had the good fortune to meet her over the phone and we were instantaneously friends. She was to become one of the most supportive people ever in my life. She made me feel safe and loved. She was the first adult that loved me unconditionally without judgment. I went into counseling to deal with the grief of her passing. She was an amazing woman and I aspire to be like her. There were over 300 people at her funeral. She played an instrumental role in my marriage. I talked to her at least once a week. She was a phenomenal cook and baker. I miss her to this day.

My former husband and I were together for 17 years. We got divorced and that is when my spiritual journey began. I can say with all honesty it was an amicable divorce. I moved into my own place. For the first time in my life I was living alone. I had my boys every other week as we had joint custody. This is when I began to unpack my emotional baggage. I went from a 9-to-5 job to a commission paying position. I knew there was going to be some stress so I started taking personal development courses. I started with a yoga class. Later I went on to become a Kundalini Yoga Instructor.

Today I still use some of the things I learned in yoga in my workshops. I felt there was something missing, so I took tap dancing and belly dancing classes. There was still a void I wanted to fill. I was listening to a lot of personal development programs and reading stacks of self-help books. I attended Tetha healing workshops and became certified in that as well. Then I did a 6-month intensive. This was the beginning of uncovering and releasing a lot of baggage I had been carrying around from when Tio Chango assaulted me. The healing began, my body started to react to a lot of foods. I became a vegetarian, then vegan. I gave up sugar, alcohol and caffeine for 3 years. The funny thing was that my body didn't release the extra weight I was carrying.

One of the exercises we did during the Intensive was to scream and cry until we felt empty inside. I lost my voice and was sick for about a week. It's amazing what our bodies/mind will do to keep us safe. I released several layers, however I still didn't feel complete. Something was still missing.

Shortly after I completed the 6-month Intensive I received a phone call telling me that Tio Chango had passed away. I decided it was time to address this terrible thing that he had done to me. I wrote several forgiveness letters and did attend his funeral. I felt such a feeling of relief. I had been avoiding family gatherings most of my adult life because I didn't want to be in the same room with him. I had been dealing with all those emotions for years. There was an intense anger phase; why didn't my parents protect me? I was very angry with my mother. Minor detour here: when I was 3 years old I was visiting my grandmother who lived down the street from our house. She gave me some bread and told me not to share. Once I got home and my mother told me to share with my brother. I had told her my grandma told me not to share, but my mother would not have it. She wet her hand and slapped me 3 times on my bottom. After being forced to share I became one to follow her rules. My mother told this story until I was forty years old. My fear and lack of voice allowed her to continue to do this. But no more!

Time kept moving and I felt numb. I hooked up with a married man I met at work. Oh heavens I cannot tell you the guilt and shame I endured for months. I was only with him the one time and never wanted to be alone with him again after that. I was miserable and now see that I wanted to punish myself.

Later someone set me up on a blind date and I was still quite naïve. I thought we would hang out talk, eat and watch a movie. I could tell he had done some type of drug. He was only interested in having sex. I was afraid and believed he could turn violent. That became my experience with date rape. He had used a condom, so I felt I was not going to get a sexually transmitted disease, but once again I felt so violated. I was in tears for days, how could I allow this to happen. I went for counseling to help me deal with the situation. My former husband called me to arrange pick for our boys and I broke down crying. I told him about the date rape and he started yelling at me. "How could you let this happen? What did you do? You must have led him on." All these judgments from him made me feel so much worse and that it was my fault. I was sitting at the Doctor's office I wanted to get checked out and wanted something to help me relax.

Looking for a way to medicate the situation rather than feel the feelings. I shared this story with a dear friend who said it was no big deal, "It happens all the time." She gave me some idea of what to do should I find myself in a similar situation in the future.

I went deeper into not feeing safe and started drinking a bit too much to mask the pain and shame. It was around this time I found meditation it made it safe for me to go into a quite space and be with myself. I also found journaling, which allowed me to write about my feelings and emotions.

In 2012, the company I worked for closed and I knew I wanted to do something different with my life and so the search began. I started attending business workshops and going to networking events. In one year I spent 165 days out of the year at workshops and trainings. I was determined to find the thing that was going to fill my void. I spent a lot of money, I chased a lot of shinning objects, I worked with a lot of coaches and did learn a great deal in the process. I do think that people are basically good and that they believe that their product or service can help your business. My biggest lesson from all of this was a cookie cutter approach does not work me. I created my own individual program that is based on where the person is and where they want to go.

I attended a three-day event, Play to Win with Clinton Swaine, in downtown Los Angeles and I started to discover my voice. He was an amazing intuitive and listener. Clinton was able to help me peel back the layers to find myself. There were times he screamed at me, but I know this was the turning point in my new adventure and journey. I took a few other courses with his organization and I started to feel confident. During one of the courses I met a very nice lady and she ended up being my Reiki teacher. I continued on this path and become a Reiki teacher, and Reiki master with her guidance. More baggage was slipping away.

I continued to attend a lot of business conferences. I wanted to get my business off the ground and make it a big success. I now know it was a way to keep myself busy so that I would not have to deal with my internal emotions. My weight persistently went up and down, and the void I was still feeling seemed to go very deep.

I NEVER thought I would become an Energy Healer. I didn't want the responsibility and was concerned about what friends and family would think of me. However, becoming a Reiki teacher opened my eyes to so many possibilities. So that internal healing continued. My teacher said one of the most important things I have ever learned; "Heal yourself first then help others shine their light." It was time for me to heal!

In September of 2017 I went to a three-day retreat and received a Starlight Attunement. This was quite the test of endurance and commitment. I was beginning to feel comfortable as a healer. I talked to a few friends and told them about my experience. As a result I started doing some healing sessions for them. In March of 2018 I got my first paying client. Yeah!

Around April of 2018 I watched a friend's Facebook live event. There were four women who had created the Yo También Healing Movement. I reached out to two of the ladies in the group to see how I could be of service in their movement. I connected with one of the ladies and we agreed to meet up in person in the near future. The Facebook live was on a Tuesday. The following day I had a class with a group and the coach asked me what I was hiding. "What are you afraid people will find out?" My first response was nothing; I'm not hiding anything. The coach went on to say "You don't need to share with the group, however be honest with yourself the truth will set you free." There it was, the target, the message on my forehead. I went back to being nine years old and Tio Chango touching me. I thought I had healed. I was sure it was over. I cried for days, confronted by many emotions.

In the form a dream, almost a download, I was guided to move Portland, Oregon in May of 2018. I had never been to or known anyone in Portland. However, my guidance leads me to move and so I did. I didn't know why I was moving to Portland I was just going. In June and July of 2018 I received three 7th Dimension Attunements. I believe this was my birthday gift from above – my birthday is in June. Receiving these 7th Dimension attunements fused all the healing modalities I had been exploring for the prior 15 years, and put all these healing gifts in to a Tiffany box with a big silver ribbon. I could no longer hide from the work I was born to do.

A couple months later on August 8, 2018, I received new instructions in the instrument of a dream. I packed up my car and started my journey to Orange County, California. I was guided to move to Orange County and host workshops for the Latino Community. The download was clear and concise that I needed to do work with my tribe. I began by working at a community 5K run and going door-to-door, encouraging people to get out and exercise their right to vote.

In September 2018, I had dinner with one of the Yo También Healing Movement's women. She shared that several members of the group were writing a chapter for a book in the hopes to create a safe place for Latino women to talk about their experiences with sexual trauma. She asked me if I would be interested in writing a chapter. In the American Indian community one of every two women is sexually traumatized. In the Latino community we don't have statistics because we don't talk about it. It is now time to talk about it.

I met with some of the authors of the book and we were all on the same page. I felt it was time to speak up and share my story in the hopes that it will allow some other girl, boy, woman, or a man to have the courage to talk about their experience and get the guidance and counseling they need to help them begin their journey into healing.

The time to heal and help others is now. No one needs to carry a secret because they never know how the secret may affect their life. I knew I wanted to write this chapter. I struggled whether I should tell my family before the book was published or wait until after. I have chosen to wait until after the book is published. I do not want their judgment and do not want to be talked out of doing this because of what other people might think.

I encourage you to seek the help you need whatever that may be for you. Check out the Yo Tombien Facebook and ask for help. I assure you, your life will be so much easier when you heal yourself and release the guilt and shame. You will have more joy and love in your life. The joy and happiness I feel now is amazing. I often laugh by myself. I'm doing the work I love and that brings me so much joy and satisfaction.

There is no one size fits all healing process. I suggest you test out several ways to release and heal yourself. Let go of your Tio Chango and be who you are meant to be without fear, shame or judgment.

The most important thing is to have compassion for yourself and allow the emotions you buried to come to the surface. The less emotions you hide the lighter you will be the more joy you will have. From my heart to yours, with love and appreciation.

"From a small seed a mighty trunk may grow."

Aeschylus

Rev. Lorraine Martinez Cook
Medicine Woman, Artist, Massage Therapist, Activist, Sacred Storyteller

She intuitively knew her life journey would lead her to the Healing Arts of a Medicine Woman. Coming from a mix of Apache, Caddo and Mexican-American ancestries she has been honored to teach the Medicine Wheel as a navigational tool to the inward journey. She became a Licensed Massage Therapist to better understand the anatomy of the human body and its stresses. A calling to become a non-denominational Ordained Minister followed her as an integral part of her being. As an artist and storyteller, her heart smiles. She lives with her husband Robert and their Pomeranian, Cookie Jean in Carson Valley, Nevada in shadow of the sacred Mountain she calls, "Sierra Madre." The journey continues.

Connect on Facebook: The Sierra'ness Way

WHERE DO WE GO FROM HERE?

We live in extraordinary times . . .

Time that creates space for extraordinary people to come together. Coming together in circle as an amelioration to our higher selves.

I was invited to step into a circle that holds great potential for healing. This circle is the Yo También Healing Movement. The courage, strength and integrity felt in the presence of these women and a gentleman was profound because change is imminent.

• • •

My life journey began in the city named after Our Lady Queen of the Angels, Los Angeles. When life switched gears I found myself residing in different cities around the globe, Dallas, Singapore and Jakarta. I found opportunity to travel the world and learn about my love for all people.

A quest to heal came while feeling opened, surrendered and vulnerable because of a family tragedy. I embarked on an inward journey and discovered the ancient medicine teachings of the Q'eros of Peru. I found comfort in the earth-based teachings of The Four Winds Society.

I continued my journey into the rainforest of the Amazon and undertook the teachings of Maestro Amador and the sacred plant medicine Madre Ayahuasca.

When I returned home it was the *Tias* (aunts) that knew I was ready to learn the teachings of my own native heritage, Mexican-American/Apache/Caddo. I continued to learn with beautiful and gracious Medicine Women along the way.

It is my personal belief and experience that we as humans have a natural tendency to collaborate with compassion. That being said, I would like to tell a sacred Story shared from Hawaiian Elders.

> "They say that the SKY FATHER had an affair with the Woman that is the SEA. She is the younger sister of the EARTH MOTHER. It is she, which came last. They say the SEA is both the eldest matron and the youngest, most innocent of maidens. This is how they talk about the SEA, the sacredness of it. How it holds the sacred Hoop of Life.
>
> It is there, in the tidal pools along the shore line that LIFE begins. Salt water is what all women carry within them. In this salt water women carry the capacity to create new LIFE.
>
> Now LIFE multiples itself in the SEA and the SEA becomes full, so very full. LIFE very slowly, very gingerly moves up onto the land. At that moment the EARTH MOTHER can reek her vengeance because of the betrayal of the SKY FATHER! The betrayal of the woman that is the SEA!
>
> However, that is not what happens?! Instead, what happens is the EARTH MOTHER embraces new LIFE and generates LIFE exponentially. So

now LIFE not only fills the ocean, it fills the LAND and the SKY. SKY FATHER can now enjoy his own creation directly.

We know that by EARTH MOTHER's act of Compassion we are here, we are alive."

There is so much that this sacred story teaches us. Take a minute to sit with it and let it inform you at a deeper level.

• • •

Dr. Anita Sanchez, in her book, "The Four Sacred Gifts," shared the Eagle Hoop Prophecy. This prophecy carries within it: Forgiving the Unforgivable, the Gift of Unity, the Gift of Healing and the Gift of Hope. In the sacred story above I found all the Gifts we need to drive our lives forward.

When we are open, when we are surrendered, when we are vulnerable we actually open a field of compassion in and around us. All nature is in these states, the flower, the forest and the lakes. All sentient life as we know is exposed to the elements, to time, to change. Yet this is where the magic happens. This is where possibility is given permission by our free will to thrive.

By the action of EARTH MOTHER in the story told, deep in her knowing she reminds us of our own ability to take *hucha* (the atomic weight of emotions) and recycle it into the earth to become fertilizer for the seeds of our becoming. Nothing is wasted.

The action of **Forgiving the Unforgivable** takes great courage, yes indeed. However we are never alone. Our greatest ally is EARTH MOTHER. She knows us better than we know ourselves. Yet we forget what easy access we have to her. All we need to do is sit down on her or be barefoot on her. Feel her with your fingertips; tell her your story as our ancient relatives told theirs to her. Feel yourself soften in her embrace. Remember she is part of the whole equation that is FATHER SKY and the WOMAN they call the SEA. They share everything. Trust her.

The second Gift of the prophecy is **Unity**. I find that there is a great disconnect to EARTH MOTHER today. So many have forgotten her in their life's journey. In our quest to compete with each other for material wealth we flat out ignore her. We look at dirt as dirty. We take the sky for granted. We see water as unsafe. We view the Sun as our enemy by wearing toxic sunscreens instead. But it is our EARTH MOTHER that unifies us all. We are made of the elements of Earth, Air, Fire and Water. We share this with all that is, all that we know, all our relatives on Earth. We call the Stone People, the Plant People, the 2-leggeds, the 4-leggeds the creepy crawlers, the Finned ones, the Furred ones and the Feathered ones our relatives. Talk about *Familia*! Re-remember we are one great big family. Find yourself in all people and smile.

The third Gift that the prophecy gives us is **Healing**. When we change our perspective the whole world looks different to us. By embracing the first two gifts, Forgiving and Unity, we prep a new landscape for healing to occur. Think of yourself as a gardener. A gardener works with the soil so that the seeds will germinate. Healing is infinite. Healings can be as great as the Pope or Dalai

Lama blessing you, if that is your thing. Healing can be as soft as someone listening, really listening without correcting you and without judgment. Healing can be climbing a steep rock face. Healing can be paint on a paintbrush and your imagination. Healing can be writing a new narrative for the next 7 Generations. Healing waits for us to re-remember our epic journey we call Life.

The final Gift is **Hope**. This is the fertile soil we plant the seed of our becoming. Hope is explained as an energetic field that surrounds us. When we summons Hope within our hearts it activates this field. It is said that women have two hearts, one in the chest and one in the belly. One we create from and one we give/receive from. How wonderful is that! Like EARTH MOTHER in the Sacred Story we find ourselves open, surrendered and vulnerable. Completed and eager to receive the seeds of our wildest dreams. The beauty of Hope not only gives to us personally, but to all our love ones a taste of inspiration. Now isn't that what we live for?

Kadeeshte, walk in beauty all the days of your life.

YO TAMBIEN
HEALING MOVEMENT

GET INVOLVED WITH THE
YO TAMBIÉN HEALING MOVEMENT

If anything in this book has touched you please help us grow our movement. We would like to see a world free of sexual abuse and trauma.

If you know anyone who has experienced trauma please share this book with them.

We would love your feedback email us at: yotambienhealing@gmail.com

CONNECT WITH US

YoTambiénHealing   @YoTambiénHeal

SOCIAL MEDIA TAGS
#YoTambién #YoTambiénHealingMovement

Cynthia Ruiz, Gabriela Torres & Jennie Estrada
Founders of Yo También Healing Movement

Made in the USA
Middletown, DE
07 May 2019